PRAISE FOR GIVE ME A MEMORY

Extraordinary courage, clarity, and humanity ... a rare and necessary contribution to the literature on complex trauma.

—Vanessa Kredler, Registered Clinical Counsellor,
New South Wales, Australia

Recommending it to my colleagues

—Dr Olwyn Johnson, The Kiwi Reading Doctor,
Wellington, New Zealand

Struggled to put it down... I wish I could more strongly convey the need for the folks in these systems (and those who make the systems) to read experiences of folks like Robyn.

—Kiefer, GoodReads review

Honest, brave, and deeply insightful... a fantastic read.

—Omri Reading, Podcast co-host/Senior Peer Supporter,
Life Matters Suicide Prevention Trust |
Te Whare Oranga Ngākau, Dunedin, New Zealand

GIVE ME A MEMORY

FACING THE PAIN OF CHILDHOOD EMOTIONAL NEGLECT: A COMPLEX TRAUMA MEMOIR

ROBYN L PARKINSON

The Husky Press

Copyright © 2025 Robyn Parkinson

Robyn Parkinson asserts her moral right to be identified as the author of this work.

All rights reserved. No part of this publication may be reproduced or transmitted in any form or by any means, electronic or mechanical, including photocopying, recording or information storage and retrieval systems, without permission in writing from the copyright holder.

Without limiting the author's exclusive rights, any unauthorised use of this publication to train generative artificial intelligence (AI) technologies is expressly prohibited.

Published by The Husky Press
www.thehuskypress.com

A catalogue record for this book is available from the National Library of New Zealand.

ISBN 978-0-473-75561-4 (paperback)
ISBN 978-0-473-75562-1 (EPUB)

With thanks to:
Martin Taylor, Digital Strategies, publishing consultant
Brian O'Flaherty, Punaromia Publications Limited, editing
Cover design: https://thedesignlounge.nz

CONTENTS

Author's note	ix
Prelude	xi
Loss	1
The void	7
Isolating	9
Living nightmare #1	17
Living nightmare #2	22
Death is not the end	31
No known cause	36
The first time	40
Sending out an SOS	43
Calling 111	54
Will it work?	59
Never a problem	64
It's mental	68
It's hormonal	73
Tears	81
The safety dragon	84
Childhood in paradise	90
Darkest after dawn	95
In living memory	103
It's on your genes	108
Waiting, again	113
In need of a little Divination	117
Would you like to come this way?	123
Ghost fighting	132
Ghostbusters	138
Back on the therapy trail	150
Diagnose or not	154
Loss eternal, loss divine	158
#5	166
#6	175

Trust	182
Ancient Dragons	191
Testing, ready or not	198
Intensity	204
Healing is not linear	208
Darkness visible	214
Fluffy Greek Hero	218
Wasting time	223
Of teddy bears and guinea pigs	226
Not this day again	229
Time warps	233
I can forget	238
More tests	245
Awareness	250
Starting over	252
A Wire Monkey Mother	265
A privileged life of trauma	269
Postscript	277
Acknowledgments	279
Bibliography	281
About the Author	283

'You can't fix what you don't acknowledge.'
— My sister

AUTHOR'S NOTE

All names except a few — mine, my husband's, and my late mother's, or those of public figures — have been changed to protect the privacy of those connected to my story. Names of all health workers and volunteers I encountered are omitted or changed, and genders changed, or a non-binary term used. There is no one individual at fault in causing my trauma. Our society has come to accept the toxic as a normal way of life.

This memoir describes severe personal psychological distress and its possible roots.

If a reader does not find at least some of it distressing, I would suggest this may indicate a need to find a good therapist. Feeling is essential to being human.

I am not telling this story for sympathy or validation or to cause distress: but I recognise that all these outcomes are likely. To my fellow survivors, I absolutely do not want to trigger you further. But I also cannot predict what you, the unique and beautiful human being that you are, will find triggering, nor know whether you have the support you need right now to read this book. I leave this decision up to you.

PRELUDE

I want, very badly, to be fixed. As quickly as possible. It feels so urgent, so necessary.

How can I possibly survive like this much longer?

I am grasping at something almost no-one around me has even heard of or experienced: not counselling, not talk therapy, not a psychologist, not a psychiatrist, not the antidepressants constantly hovering in the background of a GP visit. Until desperation made me a trauma research junkie, I'd never heard of it before. But it sounds cutting edge, well-researched, evidenced-based therapy for trauma. Apparently, it gives fast results. I look it up online and discovered there are, amazingly, people in my town who provide this mode of therapy — Eye Movement Desensitisation and Reprocessing (EMDR).*

So, I'm here. Finally. It's our fifth session together. We've

---

* Even the founder of EMDR, Francine Shapiro, would now change the name, as the bilateral movements do not need to be eye movements. She developed this in 1987. Thirty-five years, books, awards, journal articles, and training around the world, and almost no-one I know had ever heard of it. Welcome to the realm of slow-moving thought, life before the internet took off.

navigated the first session, me describing why I'm here. We gave up on session two, cut short after just twenty minutes as I went through a major panic attack, barely able to speak or breathe, shaking at home for hours afterwards. We're through session three, where I practically beg to get started on the actual EMDR process and promise to do anything needed to make this happen. I'd even brought along a printed two-page list of who the main people in my life are, annotated with notes.

At the end of that session the therapy provider holds these bits of paper in her hand and looks bemused. 'I've never had a client do this before. Thank you, this is useful.' But she continues to look a bit baffled.

One of my daughters, when told this story, laughs uproariously.

'That's you, Mum, hyper-competent even in therapy!'

The therapist is adamant that I can only start the EMDR process if I have someone to bring me to the appointment, wait for me, and be with me afterwards. And I am to provide names of backups. Just in case.

Just in case I want to end my life, again.

As we've gone over before, she asks me to briefly bring to mind a pre-selected memory. We'd agreed on a list of distressing memories from the last six months that could be processed. She's read the latest research, which suggests that starting with more recent memories is more effective than trying to process older ones. I'm impressed she's done this, and relieved she appears competent.

So now, she asks me to rate how distressed I am when thinking of this memory, how bad is it for me in the present moment? A number from 0 to 10, 10 being totally distressed and 0 being totally okay.

But I can't feel... anything. Again, like last week. What am I supposed to say? How does this work? It's beyond me to understand. The memory selected for therapy today is of *the* phone call, the one I always knew would change my life, the one that set off the four months of agony leading up to now. It's the catalyst for being here, paying $150 an hour to someone I only met a few weeks ago.

I think, therefore, that I should be feeling rather distressed. The white-grey walls and dark grey carpet of the therapist's room recede into the background as I try to focus. Hard.

'Um, it would have been 10 out of 10 on the day, I went into total shock for at least an hour... I guess it's now an 8?'

She raises two fingers from her right hand up before my eyes, forefinger and middle finger held together, the others rolled down onto the palm.

She sits on an office chair, somewhat higher than my position on a small light grey couch, and off to one side. I don't want to look at her anyway, I don't want the messiness of any actual connection with this professional trying to help me. It feels like I've been down that deadly attachment road already. I just want all my brokenness to be magically fixed. Preferably, by yesterday.

Those two raised fingers move quickly and rhythmically back and forth, back and forth, across my line of vision. I track them with my eyes, just like last session. I hope this time something will happen, that the magic will start working, that the agony of searching for and waiting for weeks and weeks will be worth it.

My breathing suddenly gets shallow and rapid, there's some kind of monster clutching at my throat and chest, and I feel... utter terror. I can't tell how long this goes on for.

The finger movements end abruptly and the arm lowers.

'Stop,' she instructs then pauses. 'Take a deep breath.' Another pause. 'What's coming up?'

'I feel... my breathing's gone funny.... I feel terrible... I never want to feel this way again!', I blurt out in rising panic, desperately not looking at her.

She pauses for the briefest of moments.

'Just notice that.'

Swiftly the arm rises, and the two fingers move rapidly once more, across my line of sight.

LOSS

*'What has happened cannot be made right.
What is lost cannot be restored...
Acknowledgement is everything.
You're in pain. It can't be made better.'*

— Megan Devine:
'It's OK that You're Not OK'

You know in your head that all it takes is one phone call to change your life.

It could be the death of a family member, a job offer, a cancer diagnosis, whatever.

Mostly humanity gets by from day to day, pretending this isn't so. Until it happens to you.

While I knew in my head my loss was very possible, I clearly hadn't allowed myself to really address or make plans for the possibility, and neither it seemed had quite a few people around me. It wasn't just a great shock to me; it was a shock to a few supporters who I looked up to and respected. And, it turns out, to a bunch of complete strangers.

One phone call. 'You weren't successful.' I've lost the election; I will not represent my local ward on the city council of my country's capital city. I lost so convincingly that the caller conveyed in the kindest way possible that there was no hope of salvation from special votes or a recount.

For about an hour the world kind of goes blank.

I go back down the hallway of my daughter's flat on autopilot. 'I didn't get in.'

I feel nothing. I'm seeing almost nothing, thinking almost nothing.

My daughter's flatmate, also awaiting results, hears his phone go off and grabs it.

The first moments of my loss are hearing someone else also lose, but his loss is clearly much closer to a win than mine, almost a mini victory. Mine is just a stark, obvious, inescapable loss. There's nothing to salvage here, no redeeming feature. Just loss.

I message my husband, who is at home isolating with COVID along with our eldest offspring.

Straight after, he messages back.

'I love you and you always will have my vote.'

Reading that out loud raises a laugh. The next generation love seeing old folks like us having a good relationship. It seems rare.

I'm still blank. I ask my daughter, 'Who else do I need to tell?' Now, before the news soon becomes public property. She mentions my recently acquired mentor, so I message her.

'Oh, Robyn — I can't believe it. Your bio read better than any of the others by a country mile. I'm soooo gutted for you. What do you need right now? Company? Food? Distraction? Peace? Love to you and Andrew.... Where r u by the way?'

I'm about to learn, over the next days, weeks, and months, how few people understand the impact as well as this, and even fewer have any idea what to do.

When the first couple of hours of shock start wearing off, I realise I am in big trouble.

The waves of grief, anger, and all-consuming emptiness are the most intense things I've ever experienced. Nothing else comes close, not the death of my parents, the untimely death of friends to tragic accident or cancer, nothing. I can feel myself imploding, the world receding. I am there, but not there.

That same afternoon I sit with my daughter at the post-election party, only to find ourselves two or three metres away from where the camera crew prepare to interview the new mayor on her landslide victory.* She is, literally and deservedly, in the spotlight. I am sitting with my daughter on black-painted low risers, unable to talk to anyone. A party member at some point comes up to ask gently if I want to give a speech. I can only shake my head. It is the exact opposite of the fear I'd carried throughout the election campaign. My worst nightmare, I had believed, wasn't me losing, but my winning and then having to work under one of the other mayoral candidates. I'd been in local politics long enough to see

---

* Tory Whanau gained the mayoralty of Wellington, the capital city of New Zealand, in October 2022 with more than twice the votes gained by any other candidate. Her lead of over 17,000 votes stood in stark contrast to the incumbent mayor, who won in the 2019 election by just sixty-two votes.

how difficult or toxic the working environment becomes when people with low leadership ability gain power. That's on top of the stories I'd heard of graphic death threats to city councillors, and a leader of my political party physically assaulted:* of going through the party Campaign 101 tutorials on how opposing factions could come after you and your past, how they have done so elsewhere. There was an ever-present sense of fear and unreality and uncertainty in the months prior to the election, held just two years into the COVID pandemic. Fear layered upon fear.

For the next few days, the rest of my household, down with COVID, keep up consolation at a distance, while I feel a little guilty about not being there for them, drowning in a sea of intense, uncontrollable emotions.

I go through the motions of the self-employed, elected person who has lost their position.

The stuff that nobody tells you how to do, for which there is no training manual, and no support. I forward emails, set up an auto-response, unsubscribe from a lot of suddenly irrelevant or irritating newsletters. There's an awkward week or so of transition. Until the results are final, you are still an elected member, even though you know you've lost.

And there were the 'consolation' messages, texts, emails.

Some were lovely. They acknowledged my loss, my distress, their distress, offered coffee, walk or company, whatever I needed. One was precious beyond measure: the sender had given deep thought to my skill set and humbly, tentatively, offered suggestions of a new kind of leadership role — 'Have you considered being a CEO of a charity or NGO? You would be the kind of leader I would like to have!' They offered to keep their eyes open.

---

* Newshub, 15 March 2019: https://www.newshub.co.nz/home/politics/2019/03/green-party-co-leader-james-shaw-confirms-small-fracture-in-eye-socket-from-assault.html

A few responses were an object lesson in toxic positivity and poor listening skills.

When someone responds with honesty to an enquiry of how you are, the worst thing you can do is not believe them. Telling you, a person staring in the face of utter misery, that you'll be fine, is not helpful. Fine is not what you're feeling, it's not what you can even imagine feeling: you just told them so. In psychology speak, it is invalidating. It denies your reality.

At the end of the week, I'm due to hold my election party. It had to be delayed due to the household COVID situation. The day after that I'm scheduled to stand up in church and preach, something I do once or twice a year. The party is set for the afternoon. There will be thirty or so supporters to face up to. I spend the morning avoiding contact with my own household, with close family who drop by to help. I'm scared, on edge.

I go outside to the greenhouse and find myself suddenly amid a living nightmare.

I sit down abruptly and can't move for an hour. It's like I'm chained to the garden seat. The world turns visibly white and foggy around me, as if it isn't quite there: and into my mind comes the most horrible, vivid image of how I can end it all. It's taunting, menacing.

I get through both these public engagements on the last remaining adrenaline I have.

And then the collapse begins to deepen.

There is a little improvement the following week, I even look at the job market and apply for a couple of positions. Despite referees of the highest calibre and profile, degrees in law and philosophy, a postgrad diploma, and a wide range of experience, neither organisation offers even an interview, and one doesn't bother to reply at all. But it feels irrelevant. The day after applying, the waves of grief and misery roll back in. I know I don't want these kinds of jobs, and I know I won't get them anyway. Female, mid-fifties, with the 'gaps' in my CV measuring more years than my 'experience'. I want so much more and can see only nothingness.

Aaron Hawkins, outgoing mayor of Dunedin, speaks publicly of his election loss as like 'a very public divorce... you have made all these long-term plans and you thought you were in this together, and then you find very suddenly that is not what is happening any more....'*

I'm sad for him, glad that someone else understands, all mixed up.

By day ten, those closest are encouraging me to consider seeing a GP. But the health system feels like the very, very last thing I consider will be helpful: I say no.

At this point, not even I realise quite how devastatingly correct I would be.

---

* Stuff article, 28 March 2024: https://www.stuff.co.nz/national/politics/local-government/130230655/aaron-hawkins-likens-losing-the-dunedin-mayoralty-to-a-very-public-divorce

THE VOID

'It is one thing to process memories of trauma, but it is an entirely different matter to confront the inner void — the holes in the soul that result from not having been wanted, not having been seen, and not having been allowed to speak the truth.'

— Dr Bessel van der Kolk: 'The Body Keeps the Score'

Exhaustion beyond belief sets in. What I start to call my shut-down response deepens and worsens. I am often finding it hard or impossible to talk to anyone, not even — or especially — those closest to me.

Overwhelming physical tension, muscles involuntarily twitching out of the blue, sudden huge sighs, sudden rapid breathing, panic attacks while out at the shops, hands clenching the trolley tighter and tighter, willing myself just to get the task done and get home.

On the brink of tears, or on the brink of an angry outburst, but neither happening. So immensely vulnerable, so lonely, needing yet fearing isolation.

An image comes vividly to mind one day when misery is at a peak.

Like a formless shadow I stand terrifyingly close to a void, a bottomless, unfillable dark hole — but then in horror I see there is no edge anymore, that the hole is me, and that I am nothing but on the brink of being the void. I am nothing but an emptiness.

An emptiness that feels too much for anyone to fill and too much for me to bear.

I am no longer, I may never have been, truly human, truly me. There is no sense of time, just endless, unendurable helplessness. Hopelessness.

I curl up in a foetal position on a bed, away from everyone, eyes shut tight, fists closing tighter and tighter, willing the universe to make this unbearable pain stop.

ISOLATING

*'People think grief slowly gets smaller over time.
In reality, grief stays the same size
And life slowly begins to grow bigger around it.'*

— Dr Lois Tonkin: cited on Instagram,
6 February 2024, @optionb

Wave after wave of things I can no longer do, or take part in, wash through my days.

I go from preaching that mid-October Sunday morning to complete inability to participate in a service, the next. I stop looking at my online news feed at all, full of post-election articles too painful to glance at: avoid looking at Facebook, full of friends and acquaintances getting on with normal life: put up any barrier I can to interactions that are triggering more pain and grief. Isolating myself from sources of pain is urgent, necessary, unquestioning.

In the fourth week after the loss, I have three further suicidal episodes. Each one is directly triggered by interactions with innocent, normal, wonderful people living lives that I admire and aspire to. I feel like I've turned into some kind of Jekyll and Hyde monster with ever-decreasing control over the sudden changes. How could positive things be so destructive to me? How could anyone but a mad person feel like this?

I accept an offer by my former-mentor-now-emergency-counsellor to be introduced to an experienced therapist, privately.

I know almost nothing about psychological trauma, but somewhere, somehow, I know I feel like I've come back from a war zone. The hypervigilance, the panic attacks, the triggering, the need to keep away from people, the fear. That's PTSD? How can I have PTSD from losing a stupid election?

I turn to YouTube, search for trauma, watch videos by therapists and psychologists, trying to make sense of it all. The therapist I am to see specialised in trauma, among other things. Something deep within knows this is important, somehow.

Then follows hundreds upon hundreds of hours reading books when I can, watching YouTube videos related to trauma. The best of them become my guides, my companions, the voices that lull me into blissful daytime sleeps, a seemingly endless source of new knowledge that might just cure me.

I do try to read something light and enjoyable.

I turn to one of my favourite young adult writers, Anne McCaffrey.

At the end of a chapter where the young heroine has just been badly injured and runs headlong into danger away from her misery at home, these words leapt off the page:

'Her last conscious thought was of misery, of being cheated of the one thing that made her life bearable...'

I finish that book but discover that anything lighthearted — Lego shows on TV, gardening programmes, whatever — just can't hold my attention.

I look at lists of distraction techniques, like having a shower or bath. I have suicidal ideation episodes in both of those places. Relaxation is rather hard to come by when things are that screwed up. It makes me cynical and unmotivated to try other things on the lists, for which there is no energy anyway. I play music loudly in the car, something I don't normally do, as it's usually too distracting. I need to distract myself now.

In a frantic self-care effort, I organise and go for regular walks with friends and acquaintances — until one week, I can't muster the motivation anymore. After a month, even my favourite distractions like landscaping at a friend's place, or going to the community garden that I helped set up, suddenly lose their joy. I start to share disturbing memories, nightmares from years ago, about my dead mother. I pull out of almost everything that my past life has to offer. There is just nothingness, no energy, no motivation.

I look for and find a precious letter with a few lines from my father, written almost thirty years ago.

Dad rarely wrote, no more than a few lines at the end of several pages from my mother, and he didn't talk of personal things. I thought he had, in this letter. On reading it I discover that for all these years, I've remembered his words incorrectly: I thought he'd written, 'I feel closer to God in the garden.' But he says nothing directly about himself or how he feels. It's impersonal. 'Most gardeners find God when working peacefully in their garden — peace and solitude!' he wrote. 'The converse is if one is tired of gardening, one is tired of living!! Sermon concluded...,' he wrote.

God, I wonder what he would have thought had he known how true that is for me now.

But Dad has been dead for decades.

My therapist, much later, responds to this story: 'Weren't you clever? You gave yourself what you needed.' It takes at least a week for this to sink in. My childhood was so emotionally impoverished, I felt the need to invent a personal connection that wasn't there?

My first thoughts of jumping off something high come three weeks post-election. This time, unlike previous suicidal thoughts, there is no immediate kickback reaction, no thoughts of, 'Oh no, I can't possibly do it that way because...'. Previously, the thoughts have been intrusive, unwelcome, unbidden visitors. Until this time. But the thoughts come and go, and other things must be done. The same day I had a video meeting with the manager of my sister's rest home. I've had to make a complaint about poor communication around her care, for the first time in fourteen years of her being there.

It is incredibly unsettling to see my behaviour change so much, and so fast. The shutdown response, not being able to speak, sometimes eases up: my husband says I'm 'making progress'. We cling to small things in an ocean of uncertainty.

I tell my husband at some point early on about the suicidal thoughts. I can't bring myself to use the actual word, 'suicidal', but he gets the drift quickly. He hadn't realised, despite his depth of concern. In trying to comprehend, his mind jumps to the Greek tale of Ajax that he is reading... hastily saying he didn't think my story would end the same way. Unfamiliar with the details of much mythology, I read it up. Ajax, the human hero with the least amount of help from the gods. Maybe that's why he ended it all: he just never learned to accept help?

Six weeks after the first episode comes my first foray into researching methods of dying. I'd had a few bad nights' sleep in a row, one thought led to another, and there I am, furtively searching the internet. In the end I write that off as one method too inconveniently uncertain in outcome to be bothered with. If I am to try to end my life, I feel I want to be sure it will work.

My emergency counsellor suggests some tools.

'Maybe try writing a letter to your mother, to your father? Say what you like?'

I manage one for my dad. To my mother? Impossible. Not in my wildest imagination can I be bothered writing to my mother. There's nothing to say that is not filled with anger. And anger was not safe in her presence. It still isn't.

'Try writing a lament?'

The next morning, at three o'clock, I write and send the result.

Loss comes
Unwelcome
Always
But not so
Death

I got the impression this isn't quite what the counsellor had in mind.

I try reading a book that I nearly couldn't bring myself to read — the title, *You're Not Broken*,[*] felt totally incorrect. I read some. I come to a part where the author gently suggests not going on to do

---

[*] Dr Sarah Woodhouse, *You're Not Broken: Break Free From Trauma and Reclaim Your Life* (Penguin Random House Australia, 2021).

the self-help suggestions if the reader has serious symptoms, but to seek professional help instead. Suicidal thoughts feel serious. I return the eBook to the library. Maybe some people with trauma can be 'not broken' enough for self-help. Looks to me like I'm not in among those lucky ones.

I am, almost inevitably, sent the 'Wild Geese' poem,* not one I'd read before, but clearly well-known and much loved by this modern poet's readers; simple, heartfelt, inspiring.

I cry. A little.

That first line — 'You do not have to be good' — spoke straight to me.

But much of the rest does not. It jars. I look it up online, discover that this poem is credited with even saving lives by giving hope to the depressed and hopeless. I read about the poet's background, and I understand rationally why the poet felt safer outside in nature, given that she was abused as a child indoors. But I feel cynical and unseen. Somehow, my childhood just wasn't that simple, even in its badness. I don't, for the most part, have bad memories of actual abuse. I learned very early on that it was physically unsafe to argue with our mother. I learned that being well-behaved was a survival mechanism, and that doing well at school got me positive attention, of a kind, a poor, watery, substitute for the real soul food of a loving, attentive, kind parent. But being outside in a suburb in the largest city in your country, there's not much chance to be consoled by nature.

Her country is not mine. I've never heard wild geese in my country.

The impulse of writers to respond to another's poem is

---

* 2004 *Wild Geese: Selected Poems*, Bloodaxe, ISBN 978-1-85224-628-0: read aloud by the author — https://www.themarginalian.org/2014/09/24/mary-oliver-reads-wild-geese/

and another NZ response poem, https://thespinoff.co.nz/books/17-02-2023/the-friday-poem-wild-geese-by-mary-oliver-by-hera-lindsay-bird-by-rebecca-hawkes-by-rebecca-hawkes centuries old. As a teenager in English class, I always found the worldly-wise, cynical response of the nymph so much more satisfying than the romanticising of Nature by the shepherd.*

Even the natural world can feel unkind.

So, in response to Mary Oliver's 'Wild Geese', I wrote this poem, 'Night Owl'.

Night Owl

You do not have to be good
But to have walked on your knees
For the hundred-mile desert of childhood
Made that path too hard to leave
You would so love to only feel your body
To love what it loves
But you cannot feel at all, or only too much
So, tell of your despair? —
you barely start, there is no time
for your bottomless pit
in the noise of another's more normal life
Meanwhile for you, the pain goes on
and on
Meanwhile the sun and rain and sky keep moving
across the tree ferns, kōwhai, tawa, and wild cherry trees
Meanwhile the fantail sports by your window
and the morepork calls alone in a long clear night
uncaring whoever you are if you hear
Over and over announcing no place
For you, no family, nothing, —
A void.

---

* See the Wikipedia article: https://en.wikipedia.org/wiki/The_Nymph%27s_Reply_to_the_Shepherd

Around the same time, I write a response to Leunig's 'Wish List' poem.*

We had just gone whale-watching at Kaikōura.

In my state, it was underwhelming to be packed a hundred or so tourists to a boat, hyped up with videos of close-up shots of impressive whales, only to get a few bare glimpses from a respectful distance of a tail, two, perhaps three minutes' sighting at max for a three-hour trip. I thought of the amount of fossil fuel used by these tourist boats. This is not the way to see the majesty of the natural world, and once more nature fails to be a magic fix. I'm a monster, I think. Other people love this whale-watching thing. It's an international tourist attraction. I'm that broken.

I find some consolation in the poet Leunig's fall from grace.† Which also makes me broken, I guess. So, I write another response poem, 'Reality List'. I haven't written this many poems since schooldays.

Reality List

Sanity, questions, well-wishing, 'care'
Not so simple past a prayer
Texts, messages, baking, 'peace',
Poems on trauma and wild geese.
Trees and flowers, grass and seeds
All faded to a mind that bleeds.
Cups of tea and ocean swell
Whales and beaches, none can quell
This endless ache for kindness, care
On a garden path that leads nowhere

---

* Australian cartoonist, Michael Leunig: https://www.leunig.com.au/works/recent-cartoons/816-wish-list
† https://www.news.com.au/finance/business/media/cartoonist-michael-leunig-axed-from-prime-spot-at-the-age-over-offensive-vaccine-image/news-story/3b6b99a4101ebe53df58cb21827dfod4

LIVING NIGHTMARE #1

'Trauma is perhaps the most avoided, ignored, belittled, denied, misunderstood, and untreated cause of human suffering.'

— Dr Gabor Maté and Daniel Maté: 'The Myth of Normal: Trauma, Illness, and Healing in a Toxic Culture'

I've had two 'worst nightmares' in my life, and both have come to pass.

In my third year as a Scarfie,* in the late 1980s, I lived with four friends in a typical student flat. Old, cold; dodgy floorboards in the toilet. In a fit of economising, I'd organised this move from our previous year's brand-new flat, close to lectures, to this. Cheaper but not cheerful. I tried painting the dull green walls of my tiny room but knowing nothing about choosing colours, ended up with an overwhelming shade of pink. Perhaps not out of place in other kinds of working bedrooms but truly hideous in this confined area with high ceilings. Despite lovely flatmates it wasn't a great experience, and I organised a move back to the new flat the following year with some of them. I was nineteen.

One day that year in the old house, a knock comes at the door. I can't recall who opened it.

My sister Tina is standing there.

She is meant to be over a thousand kilometres away, in Auckland.

In Carrington, a psychiatric hospital.† She is so glad to see me: I am terrified to see her.

I am terrified of the responsibility, of the weight of needing to do something, of not knowing or wanting to do anything. I'd left everything behind very willingly to go to university for a degree I could have done in my hometown. By this stage I no longer went 'home' for the summer holidays but stayed and worked in Dunedin, visiting only briefly for Christmas.

I thought I had left behind — everything.

---

* 'Scarfie' is the term for a university student at Otago University in Dunedin, where it is far enough south — nearer the Antarctic — that a scarf in winter is just about a necessity.
† Formerly the Auckland Lunatic Asylum, this institution opened in 1865 and closed in the deinstitutionalisation of care by the early 1990s, just a few years after my sister's escape.

Tina comes in. We talk. I establish she doesn't have any medication with her.

I ring Carrington Hospital.

'My sister Tina is here. I'm in Dunedin. She says you took away her clothes and made her wear pyjamas.'

'We did that to stop her running away.'

'Well, she's here, and she says she doesn't like that.'

I don't recall stating the obvious, but it hung in the air: my sister has not just 'run away'. She has managed to find her confiscated clothes from the health professionals, and her bank book; leave the hospital, go to a bank, withdraw all her savings, get to the airport, fly over a thousand kilometres to Dunedin, get to my flat from the airport. This is 1988. There is no widespread use of the internet or cell phones, and yet she's achieved this.

Their management strategy does not appear to be working well.

I ask for medication details; I say that I'll try to persuade Tina to return.

It occurs to me that this nurse doesn't know anything about me — that I'm only nineteen, eight years younger than my sister, that I'm in a student flat, that I have no older adults around to turn to in this situation.

The conversation finishes. I hang up.

Tina wants me to take her shopping. She wants to buy a cross and a bible. I remember we managed to find them, but the rest of that afternoon visit is blanked out from my memory. She agrees, much more readily than I expected, to return to Auckland. It's a huge relief.

We must have arranged a shuttle to the airport, and back at my flat, there's time to fill in. I curl up on the lounge floor and nap. It is an effort to block out the reality, the overwhelming reality that I can't just leave my past behind.

After a while my flatmate gently shakes me awake with concern in her eyes: 'Your sister is needing you.'

I somehow had known this day would come. Because my sister,

if she ever wanted to escape a psychiatric unit, would want to go as far away from it as possible. Would want to see me, not our parents, who lived just an hour's drive north of Auckland. Not coincidentally, I was about as far away as possible from our parents as I could be and still go to university in my country of birth. Not one of my friends from high school even contemplated doing the same. It was not common to come across another Aucklander in Dunedin for university.

I'm stuck, frozen. I can't help my sister, and somehow, instinctively, I don't think she's getting the right help. The voice on the phone at the hospital has no compassion or understanding. At one point when hearing that the visit is going better than I expected, the voice alters with a false, sickly-sweet tone.

'In fact, you're quite enjoying it!' she exclaims hopefully, triumphantly, as if saying it will make it so.

'Umm.... no, I wouldn't say that.'

I wonder whether this person is living on the same planet as me.

This is my worst nightmare come true — having to be responsible for someone but unable to help or function, totally unprepared and ill-equipped, stuck in terror. Having Tina escape a psychiatric ward to come see me. It's not about her, it's not her fault, and to have my vulnerable sister as a nightmare scenario also feels off.

I might want to rescue my sister: but I know I can do nothing of use.

I've known that all my life.

Over half her life and most of mine is already a disastrous, terrifying nightmare of her appalling psychiatric 'care', inappropriate medication dosages, most likely incorrect diagnoses, cigarettes handed out by psychologists, hospitalisations, ECT, abuse by staff, multiple suicide attempts. I grew up witnessing and hearing things related to her 'illness' and 'care' that make a grown-up's stomach turn. I heard more as an adult.

I saw my sister Tina lose bladder control as a young teen, back from the psych ward on a break, drugged up like a zombie, eyes staring into nothingness, standing stock still on the carpeted hallway of our family's home. I saw our mother respond in disgust, not compassion. I heard, later, that Tina had been raped by a hospital orderly on the ward. I asked her nearly fifty years later.

It was not a faded memory to her. 'He was disgusting. Mum and Dad knew, but they didn't make a complaint, because they didn't want it in the newspapers. It was like torture being in that ward; they gave me shock treatment...'. My sister qualifies as a survivor of abuse in care: but she didn't even know an investigation had been going on and had not heard any apology. I rang to tell her: 'Tina, the prime minister of this country has stood up in Parliament and said what happened to you and so many others should never have happened, that is a shameful thing our nation let happen to children and vulnerable people.'* I'm not sure she could take it in. She sees herself, as many survivors do, as in some way deserving bad treatment for being a 'difficult' teenager.

As chilling as the Abuse in Care inquiry is, as large the number of survivors — an estimated 250,000 in a present-day population of five million — there is a larger truth being ignored here: not all childhood trauma survivors were abused 'in care', by the state or school or church group. For many, it happens at home.

When the grown-ups of the time who are meant to take care of you and your siblings make it clear that they can't, there is nothing left to do but get away, as far away as possible. And try to forget everything.

---

* 'The State was supposed to care for you, but, instead, many of you were subjected to the most horrendous physical, emotional, mental, and sexual abuse...[we] failed you in the worst possible way': https://www.parliament.nz/en/pb/hansard-debates/rhr/combined/HansDeb_20240724_20240724_24

LIVING NIGHTMARE #2

*'Traumatic memory is not primarily stored as a narrative event that
we can talk about.
Instead it is primarily stored as symptoms.
As emotions. As beliefs.
As tendencies. As reflexes.
As gut reactions. As things we avoid, or things we panic at.'*

— Carolyn Spring: Instagram, 16 May 2024,
@carolynspringwriter

My other worst nightmare happened eighteen years after my sister's escape from a psych ward.

And this time, I made it happen myself.

I chose, but it didn't feel like a choice. I didn't think, then, that I could do anything else and still live with my conscience. I felt trapped.

It was 2006. I flew up to my mother's home north of Auckland and my sister June flew out from Canada to help. We were there to sort out our mother's affairs, to get her into a rest home. A rest home in Wellington where I lived, not Auckland, where our sisters Liz and Tina lived. Because how could I escape this any longer? If a parent needs help, and you're the most able one, aren't you supposed to step up? How could I put our mother into a rest home in Auckland knowing that she would continue to call Tina for a daily, near-hour-long emotional dumping session? Tina, who herself needed support, who was on psychiatric drugs long term. And certainly not Liz, now diagnosed formally with multiple sclerosis, using a walking stick while only in her fifties, who had for as long as I can recall been identified by our mother as having a 'difficult, distant' relationship with her. For which our mother had theories, of course, none of them involving any accountability on her part.

No, now I believed I had to step up, so our mother needed to come to a rest home in Wellington. This was my worst nightmare, I was making it happen, and no-one around me queried whether this was a good idea.

Wellington was far enough away from Auckland to have been a sanctuary for me. Eight hours' drive, or a plane ride and difficult transport at the other end. My husband and I bought a house, had four children — three at school and one at preschool, at that time. My mother had visited only a few times over those years, averaging about an operation a year for the twelve years after her husband died — back, hips, ankles, cataracts.

That last week in our mother's house was very tense. She was in panic mode, having had one too many falls living alone, now suddenly and fully convinced she couldn't do it anymore and needed to be looked after in a rest home. I had seen this coming for over a year, had raised the issue with her of which town she'd be in 'if' the time came, planting the seed so that she felt it was her choice to come south. None of this helped me feel better about my choice, or lack of it. There was no internet support group to raise the possibility of no contact, or low contact, or just to affirm that other folk also had mothers they couldn't stand to be near. Not yet.

First, we had to get her assessed. We waited in suspense in the living room, anxious, hoping our mother had enough points ticked off to warrant being in care. The assessor set our fears at rest — the only question was whether our mother needed hospital level or just rest home-level care.

Then, we had to find a vacancy. There was one, just a suburb away from where I live in Wellington. Vacancies were hard to find. I'd visited a couple of rest homes already. There was relief.

Then came the rapid unravelling of years of a life lived independently. We only had a week, and too much to do.

June and I made lists, stacked boxes, contacted rubbish removers and furniture movers and real estate agents. We went through each room, working out what had to come to my house in Wellington for further sorting, what was rubbish, what might stay with the house for sale. My mother's bed, drawers, and favourite armchair could come with her to the rest home. Nothing else.

The chest freezer in the garage was the first reality check. It was full of food, of course. Our mother loved to cook, hated waste, and hated being without even more. We lunged down to the bottom with our arms outstretched and came up with wire baskets full of food from as old as twelve years ago. All neatly labelled and dated. In our surprise we exclaimed out loud. There was a wail from the lounge where our mother sat as we worked, hearing us, unable not to be in control. She wailed about the waste, as we'd said it would need to be thrown out.

'Well, you can eat it if you like, but it might kill you,' I responded.

I didn't have the energy to be sympathetic. Or the motivation.

The next shock came in the kitchen. We opened an old Tupperware container, full of flour. It moved. June and I looked at each other and knew we couldn't say a word. We dumped the weevilly flour out into a rubbish sack, without our mother knowing. We couldn't handle any more oversized wailing. We couldn't wail, no matter how much we might want to. Expressing our distress to our mother had never worked in childhood. There was no reason to think this had changed. Only her emotions mattered.

June booked a flight to accompany our mother down to Wellington at the end of the week, as the rest home could take her straight away, and she felt as desperate not to live alone anymore just as much as she had once previously been very independent. I flew back earlier, back to my world that was about to be ripped away from me, a sanctuary no longer. My second of two worst nightmares was about to happen. My mother was going to live in the same town as me, and was going to expect to interact with me, daily. For the rest of her life. She was only seventy-seven, young to go into a rest home. I thought she would live for ten more years. I tried to block the horror of that thought.

I drove to meet June and our mother at the rest home. They arrived later than expected. On this cold, grey, rainy, wintry Wellington day, our mother hadn't been able to properly convey the rest home location, and the confused driver whose English was not up to this had gone elsewhere first. We did our best to settle her in, but as always, her expectations were much higher than reality. The rooms were very small. The bed was jammed against one wall. We did what we could, then escaped for the night, driving back to my house.

On the way home, gloomy and raining, I came to a stop at the intersection bordering my home suburb and the next. There was an abrupt bang. A white van loomed at our rear. My car had been rear-ended by a young tradesman who wasn't driving to the conditions.

I've been driving now for thirty years and never been rear-ended before or since that evening.

The universe was telling me loud and clear: there was never going to be anything easy about having our mother in the same town.

As expected, my mother called on the landline I'd set up for her in her rest home room.

She called every day, expecting to talk non-stop for anywhere up to an hour.

The only thing I could say to end the torrent was to mention that I needed to go to the bathroom. That she understood, and she got off the phone at once. Any other reason required at least ten more minutes of her trying to keep dominating the conversation, unwilling to stop talking, and me trying to wrestle the conversation to the floor. It was exhausting and stressful beyond belief.

Some years later in sorting through her paperwork, I came across the hospital discharge sheet for one of her many operations. Buried in the middle of this medical language was one word I well understood: our mother had been described, by a medical professional, as 'garrulous'. Someone who doesn't stop talking.

I've had a horror of being anything like our mother, all my adult life.

Once when my youngest child was in her early teens, or at least preteen, I started to tell her a story about something that had happened to me. We were standing in the kitchen. She gently let me know I'd already told her that story. My eyes widened in horror, and I apologised, aghast, saying I didn't want to be like my mother. My daughter reminded me of this scene years later when trying yet again to convince me that I certainly wasn't like my mother.

People used to come away from a face-to-face visit with our

mother somewhat glassy eyed, in shock. They usually didn't go back. Phone calls were likewise fraught with the probability of being stuck listening to a long, long monologue. I heard from my sister that a long-standing family friend chose not to call our mother to say farewell on her departure to Wellington, just because she knew what the phone call would be like. It took me nearly twenty years for the penny to drop that grown adults couldn't handle being around our mother and if given a real choice, chose not to: but that I, like my siblings, had no such choice while we were children. We were stuck with the unspeakable horror of living with someone who had no idea of, and no desire to be aware of, her own impact on other people.

As I hoped, for Tina's sake, the moment our mother came to Wellington, she stopped calling her.

This caused a difficulty that I had not anticipated: Tina, while relieved not to be dumped on every day, had come to see those calls as at least a sign she was needed and loved. Now, it was like she didn't exist to our mother. I mumbled an explanation that Mum was very conscious of the cost of toll calls. In these still pre-smartphone days, calling someone on the phone outside of your free calling area — usually your town — felt expensive. Mother never even mentioned wanting to call Tina. Calls to me were more convenient to her, because I was the one who could run errands for her or listen to her complaints and larger-than-life stories.

To our mother's credit, she had repeated several times that she did not want or expect to be looked after in old age by any of her children, in their own homes. She told us the story of growing up in the small southern town of Timaru, before the time of rest homes, when aged parents came home to their adult offspring's houses, to sit by the fire, and to die. She saw the tension and pressure this placed on marriages, she said, and didn't want to do that to her children. But it never once occurred to her that she had exactly that same kind of impact, all my life, even from just living in the same town.

This unspeakable disconnect, this potential for empathy without any reality, knowing our mother had enough awareness to see the negative impacts of other people's behaviours, of other people's dogmas, but none for her own. She proudly told the story multiple times of debating with anti-abortionists in the 70s, apparently silencing them by making it personal and asking if they were themselves prepared to bring up someone else's child if they weren't prepared to allow abortions. But she herself was emotionally unprepared to bring up her own children, unwilling to look after us unless we were completely healthy, compliant, and undemanding. I cannot believe she would ever have herself chosen to look after anyone else's child. When the time came for one of my sisters to have an abortion, our mother was never told. There would have been wailing and emotional drama, and no support for either having or not having the child, because our mother would have been drenched in shame and unable to see who mattered most in this scenario.

There were some tools open to me as an adult, and I grasped at them as if drowning. I signed us up for the Caller ID service on our landline within the first week of my mother living in Wellington. It gave me a slight semblance of control. At least I could see it was her calling.

I only answered the phone when I had some degree of emotional resilience, or at least, resignation. This caused our mother quite some consternation. She happily talked and talked and talked down the phone line, knowing it was just the answer machine. A robot would have made the perfect companion for her. But answer machines have time limits for messages, and she got cut off. Then she rang back, angry and resentful, yelling at me via the answer machine that I needed to ring Telecom; it wasn't right that they cut her off, and I was paying for their service. Explaining to her later that answer machines were made for leaving brief messages didn't console her much. I did try to answer at least once a week, in addition to visiting once a week. Each contact filled me with unspeakable dread.

At the end of one visit, I checked in with the rest home manager for a quick debrief and mentioned the phone call debacle. She looked sideways at me as if I was rather naive.

'Quite a few of our residents haven't been given the phone number for their families,' she said.

But it was too late for me, because our mother certainly did know our number, and she was showing no sign of memory loss. It helped to know that someone understood and would have accepted my need to not be called by my own mother. It seemed then like almost no-one else had this experience. I did have one older friend from church who also had her mother in a rest home around that time. She warmly, firmly, and wisely told me, 'Robyn, when I go visit my mother, I must pray first for the strength to do so. And I must pray again afterwards. Every time.'

Decades later, my sister June asked, 'Why did you move Mum down from Auckland?'

After I explained, she said, 'I couldn't have done that. Our family is lucky you were around.'

It didn't feel lucky at all to me.

It felt like a choice to be tortured that I should never have had to make.

Visiting the rest home was made much more bearable when my youngest, then a preschooler, was with me. Then, my mother was distracted by her, and much less likely to spend the whole visit in emotional dumping. It also limited the visit time. My youngest has fond memories of these visits — not any interaction with her grandmother, as this was pretty much non-existent, but because she was given fizzy lemonade by the staff and given longing looks of attention by all. Children are not frequent visitors on weekdays in residential care settings.

Getting my mother to come to our place was difficult. Our van-like vehicle was bought for ferrying four children, not a mobility-impaired person, and the step was too high. I tried buying a medical footstool, but that was too narrow. I asked a retired man at church, and he kindly custom built a wooden step platform, wide enough and stable. So now, we had to bring my mother into our home again, on occasion.

Mother loved these outings. She raved about anything we put in front of her to eat — even simple salads that she loved and never got in the rest home. But the undercurrent of tension was always there. She wasn't just stressed about being potentially physically dependent, which for me, having no care experience of adults, was daunting enough. I carried with me the memory of one of her last visits to us some years before, when on the last day, I had gone out for a short errand trip, only to find on return that she had slipped, dislocated her hip, and required hospitalisation. We did what we could, putting grab bars in the toilet, handrails up the three steps to our front door. While physical aids helped, nothing could take away the tension I constantly felt in her presence.

She was totally emotionally dependent. Everything revolved around her, as if our worlds came to a stop when she was in the room. She said lovely positive things — 'There's love in this house! Not like at the rest home' — but the tone was desperately needy, sickly, childish, and overwhelming to me. There was a horror to it, seeing an adult act emotionally like a toddler, but knowing they have an adult's power and presence, knowing nothing I could do would alter their behaviour.

The worst part of this worst nightmare happened unexpectedly soon.

DEATH IS NOT THE END

'... the vast majority of traumatized people we see in clinical practice have been severely hurt in the context of their own families...'

— Elizabeth K. Hopper et al.: 'Treating Adult Survivors of Childhood Emotional Abuse and Neglect'

Two and a half years after my mother moved to the rest home, I received a call on my cell phone from Wellington Hospital.

'Your mother has come here from the rest home; she's had a major stroke.'

The implication was I should come visit.

'Oh.' I paused. I asked for more details.

'Okay — well — we're several hours' drive out of town this week, with friends, the wife is having cancer treatment, and we promised her a lift to another town for radiotherapy... we'll visit when we get back.' I was relieved. I could put off the inevitable hospital visit. I put out of mind what would happen then. I still believed, even though it was a major stroke, that my mother had years left of rest home life. That I had years left to endure.

I let my sister in Canada know.

Back home a week later, I rang the hospital. Mother had been transferred to a rehabilitation ward in the local hospital just a few minutes away from our home.

I visited. Her speech was badly impaired, but it took more than just one major stroke to knock out that ability. I couldn't understand everything she said. She clearly recognised me and looked glad to see me. I resigned myself to daily visits.

Then another call a week or so later — another major stroke, perhaps more than one. Other functions were deteriorating, eating and drinking becoming difficult. I updated my sister who decided to fly out, as this looked like our mother's time was up.

June's first trip to the hospital did not go well: our mother didn't appear to recognise June, thought she was a staff member, and tried to say that she wanted her facial hair removed. Her words were almost indistinguishable, but the gestures made it clear. What mattered to her most was how she looked, not who was there.

The next day, we could see more deterioration and the ability to talk seemed finally gone. But this time, our mother's face lit up in astonished recognition at seeing June's face: June seemed teary and relieved to be seen. I was surprised. Why was this so important to June? I'd happily not be recognised — that would mean no emotional pressure to be the good and dutiful daughter. When it came to our mother, I would have given anything to be totally unseen. Preferably, to not have a mother at all.

Hospital staff had about that time used the word 'palliative'. We understood, and accepted, but this wasn't the view of the doctor in charge of this rehab ward. The big man did weekly ward visits, so it had been days since he last saw our mother, and he insisted on another attempt at feeding her. The last attempt the day before had been distressing and futile, a choking risk more than any use at getting food down. June and I stood on one side of our mother and the doctor in charge on the other, and I argued. Loudly. And in vain — the feeding attempt went ahead, even more futile than before. Not that the doctor himself got to do this. No, that task falls to a nurse.

In a few days, the last phone call came. It was early morning on a school day.

'Come as soon as you can,' the nurse said. 'Your mother will die today.'

Slightly shocked, we decided to all go, the kids for a quick goodbye then off to school, June and Andrew and I then planned to keep watch.

The kids were wide-eyed. None of us had visited anyone dying before. We didn't know what to expect. A passing nurse took one look at our four children and teared up, imagining most likely that they were about to lose a loved grandmother. Our kids had no real memories of her and no relationship. She'd never really tried to interact; she would just look at them as if they were some kind of cute doll, there for her entertainment.

Mother sat upright in the hospital bed, her eyes closed. Her breathing was loud, laboured and rattling: this, a nurse explained, was how she knew death would come today. She explained that a person at this point could still hear us.

But there was nothing much to say, certainly not to our mother. We sat for several hours, sometimes we talked to each other. There was nothing we could say to her: no words of love, no acknowledgement of what she meant to us, as I expect many people do at their mother's deathbed. In dying as in living, we spared her the truth that she could not face — that she was not someone we ever wanted to be near.

The nurse popped in and explained we should not be surprised if there was another 'breath' after the moment of death — this would just be air leaving the body, not a real breath. I was so very, very grateful for this nurse's explanation. It helped then, and it helped just a year later at the deathbed of a younger friend.

We were there for the last breath; the blood drained from our mother's face; a last exhalation of air left her body, just as the nurse had described.

Her life was over. Not, for us, its impact.

There were the usual stresses of organising a funeral, removing her possessions from the rest home on a day pouring with rain. By this stage my eldest sister Liz was in residential care herself, in her mid-fifties, with multiple sclerosis. She came down with her supportive friend for the funeral. Liz had, wisely, declined the opportunity offered by this friend to come down while our mother was dying. Our other sister came from Auckland too, and we four were together, something that hadn't happened for many years. But my focus was on getting through. I wrote and delivered the only eulogy. There weren't many attenders. I focused on our mother's life history. Not one word was said about her relationship with any of us. The lovely Anglican priest, however, knew our mother well enough by now to tell a more authentic tale.

The priest told of how he'd come on a Wednesday morning to the lounge at the rest home, to lead a midweek communion service. And always, my mother was there, keen and eager.

But one day she wasn't, so he went in search of her, and found her asleep in the main lounge. He gently tried to shake her awake, knowing how much she wanted to be at the church service, saying 'Shirley, Shirley'.

To his surprise Shirley woke up in a state of great excitement. He quickly realised that she thought she'd died and gone to heaven, and that Jesus was calling her name.

He wryly commented that he had the hard job of letting down her high expectations, that he wasn't Jesus, and she was still alive for another day in the rest home, not in heaven. He commented, in a remark clearly aimed at me and my siblings, that Shirley always had very high expectations that couldn't possibly be met.

To have our experience confirmed, to have someone else state out loud in public in effect how overbearing and difficult to manage she was, helped. But, unfortunately, I and my family were then at another church, and I never met this lovely, kind, insightful man of God again.

For about a year after my mother died, maybe once a month or so, the nightmare would come while asleep. I dreamed that somehow my mother had come back to life, only to relive those last few unbearably tense weeks of daily visits, over and over. In my dream I felt, oh, so trapped. Witnessing her death seemed to make no difference. I told very few about these dreams, or my lack of tears and grief. There was no relationship to grieve except the one I'd never been given, and I had no idea yet just how important that kind of grief was. And I could tell this wasn't a normal reaction to the death of a parent. It was odd, different: I felt alone and isolated, and didn't consider reaching out for help.

NO KNOWN CAUSE

'The more healthy relationships a child has, the more likely he will be to recover from trauma and thrive. Relationships are the agents of change and the most powerful therapy is human love...'

— Dr Bruce Perry: 'The Boy Who was Raised as a Dog'

I received two phone calls after my mother died, that I remember.

One, very welcome, from my aunt Cate, my mother's sister. Her health wasn't great, and she lived far away down south, so she hadn't come to the funeral.

Cate's call was welcome because she didn't bother with any ridiculous talk about us missing her. She wondered aloud to me, deeply puzzled.

'Why was Shirley like that?'

We both knew exactly what 'that' meant.

'Our mum wasn't like that. Why was *she*?'

I explained the current theory by one of the wider family, that probably my mother had had an undiagnosed head injury. There was a fall from an upper storey window, as a young girl, and a history of back pain and two surgeries for that as an adult. Back in the 1940s no-one would have considered head injury, and nothing most likely could have been done anyway.

But I am dubious about this theory, because of the way my mother told the story about falling out of the window, and her relationship with her sister Cate.

There was almost a five-year age gap, and no other siblings. Shirley had been born nearly two years after her parents married. In the early twentieth century, this reproductive history most likely meant either miscarriages, fertility issues, illness, or perhaps an unhappy marriage. From what I knew, the marriage was a happy one with each daughter much wanted. Perhaps fertility was an issue. I don't know.

Shirley's fall from the window was a key life story she liked to repeat, at length. She would tell how she was in bed, recovering from some childhood illness. It was the early 40s and standard practice was lengthy bed rest. With an active intelligent mind but — I would conjecture — low emotional control, this clearly grated. Mother described leaning out the window, looking from her upper-storey bedroom down the quarter-acre section below. Her parents were there, most likely gardening, as growing most or all the family vegetables was still the norm in a suburban section. Cate, I think then about seven, was there too, and had her sister's toy. This upset big sister Shirley so much that she leaned out and out, yelling to get her toy back, to get attention: she leaned so far, she fell, bounced on a lean-to roof below, and landed on her back on a concrete path.

Mother also used to talk, less often, about Cate as a baby and a younger sister.

'Other adults didn't know then to give the older sibling any attention,' she would say.

'Cate was the pretty one, the intelligent one. They gave her all the attention and none to me.'

That was probably true. But her jealousy wasn't something she hid, or felt any embarrassment about; it wasn't something she even identified as jealousy or thought she had any role in. She had lost being the centre of attention from her parents and from others at age five, clearly resented it — and still felt the same way decades later, as an adult.

While at first I recall having some sympathy for my mother, there was something about the way she would keep telling this story, something creepily ominous. Surely by the age of twelve, most kids might well still feel lonely and resentful at being stuck in bed — but not to the point of being oblivious to the risk of falling out a window. To me this felt like the action of a toddler, maybe a five-year-old, not a preteen. And surely by your late fifties, you would have sorted through the emotional baggage, the undercurrent to this story?

But I could be wrong. Maybe it was just a head injury. Or maybe my mother was narcissistic, as one therapist suggested. In the end, if it was something she didn't pass on to me, I didn't care. Knowing a label or a cause would change nothing. My mother was simply, bemusingly, toxically, like 'that'.

And there, on a good day when I have some energy to catch up with long-left chores, among some yet-to-be-filed papers, is a scrap of notebook paper in my mother's handwriting. She always wrote in all caps. In her handwriting as in everything else, her life shouted at you. The note is a draft, the start of putting her orthopaedic history on paper. She clearly states she was seven years old when the accident happened, not twelve as I remembered.

Even so, seven still feels a little old to be falling out of windows. And the repeated, detailed, emotionally unaware storytelling of it, all her adult life.

Another phone call came from the widow of an uncle that I am sure I have never met. He had died the year we came back from Jamaica, when I was six. I got the impression my dad didn't approve of him, perhaps as my dad valued fidelity to marriage vows very highly, and this brother had divorced and remarried. The second wife recognised the unusual surname from the death notice in the newspaper. And proceeded, not to talk about my mother or offer condolences, but to relate how 'odd' my father's side of the family was.

On reflection I think there is more than enough neurodiversity, autism, and tragedy in my father's line to explain any 'oddness'. It seemed ironically odd that a family member I'd never met wanted not to offer any condolence but to offload about the other side of the family. Who was the truly odd one here — her husband, or herself? She seemed keen to meet up. I thought about it and decided against it. I have so little living family connection anyway. I could do without this one.

THE FIRST TIME

'We need connection with another human being to survive ... basically, Freud was wrong, sex and aggression are not the biggest instincts.'

— Dr Sue Johnson: YouTube, 'Using Attachment Theory', Being Well podcast, 15 May 2023, @Forrest Hanson

Towards the end of my third year at university, life felt like it began to unravel.

I felt depressed.

I reached out for help, the first time in my adult life, to Student Health.

Doctors at Student Health in late 1980s New Zealand seemed to have one main goal, and that was to make sure female students were on the pill. I described feeling miserable, unmotivated: I was asked if I was sexually active, and given a prescription for the contraceptive pill. Despite answering 'No'. Nothing else was offered except another appointment.

Inadvertently Student Health was on to something: I realised shortly after my visit that my emotional malaise was cyclical. But I took the pill. I didn't go back to Student Health. There seemed little point.

And there followed one of the best years of my life.

For a short while I played on a friend's indoor cricket team. In an extremely rare time of interaction, my dad had taught me the basics of bat and ball and rules of regular cricket, but I'd not had the chance to play — there was no girls team in my last year of high school. Here in indoor cricket, in mixed teams, I astonished myself and others by my effectiveness. I was such an accurate but horrifically slow bowler that male batters were baffled: caught behind, bowled, LBW. In my second game I got a hat-trick.

As my friend and her flatmate walked away afterwards with me, my friend suddenly realised she had been holding a teammate's engagement ring for him to keep it safe. She raced back to find him, leaving me and her flatmate alone, briefly. We had met once previously, at the end of my first year of university, him sporting bright red curly hair, a bright deep-pink home-knit jersey, and what seemed to me like all the typical brashness of a commerce student. There was no attraction that day.

A couple of years later at their flat, I realised he was reading a work of classic literature. Intrigued, I asked to borrow it, in the hopes this would lead to something more. I was rebuffed, in his abrupt unthinking way. It was a library book that he didn't want to on-lend, but this wasn't explained till much later.

So, the next year, walking away from our indoor cricket match, I didn't expect any bid for connection. But it came, an urgent request to come to a movie with him — urgent, I realised, as he didn't want his flatmate to know he'd just asked her friend out on a date.

Less than a year later we were married.

SENDING OUT AN SOS

'*Trauma trains us to be in amber or red — we need to train our bodies instead to be in green, and as with all training that takes time and persistence. Medication and other substances can help in the short-term but don't enable us to grow the neural networks needed for emotional regulation, so can keep us stuck, replicating merely the numbness of the red zone.*'

— Carolyn Spring: 'Why the Symptoms of Trauma Make Sense', blog for 22 September 2021, www.carolynspring.com

'It's okay not to be okay.'

'Your mental health matters.'

'Reach out and ask for help if you need it.'

Mental health campaigns and promotional material are difficult to get right.

An awareness week has run every year in New Zealand since 1993.

As the Mental Health Foundation of New Zealand acknowledges, a simple campaign, focusing on small steps everyone can take for their mental health, can feel belittling to those in actual severe mental distress; that there are real improvements needed to services and systems.*

Such campaigns in New Zealand often seem to focus on sports stars or other celebrities. People who've already experienced a high degree of success and respect, visible at a national level, who have achieved their dreams. Those feel like a light year away from my reality. Campaigns have, rightly, tried to destigmatise talking out about mental health issues, trying to educate us all that it's okay to reach out for help. But there's a problem or two with this.

Acute or chronic psychological distress doesn't listen or respond to campaign slogans, and reaching out for help is only ever okay if that help exists, is accessible, and matches your needs. It's like the marketing campaign has changed, but the product and availability hasn't. It's madness. One health worker I speak to says the sector was still operating at funding levels from over six years ago — pre-COVID — and the funding hadn't taken into consideration the increase in demand even from those public health campaigns, year after year.

In the third month after my election loss, it dawns on me with horror that the summer holidays are upon us. This is the time of

---

* https://mentalhealth.org.nz/our-campaigns/mental-health-awareness-week

year in our southern hemisphere Christmas-with-summer holiday bundle when normal patterns of life are disrupted, people go on extended vacations over a six-week period, services are sometimes maintained at a bare minimum.

It had been a pretty good few weeks up till then. I'd had no recurrence of suicidal thoughts, I'd been able to find a trauma therapy practitioner for EMDR, I'd had my intake session with her.

I ask for an estimate of how many sessions I might need. She replies that if it's through the public system, their limit is six sessions, but she finds in private practice the average is about ten. It's $150 a session, but if that gets me fixed, I feel it will be worth it.

And then one morning, the expected but unwelcome news comes of the death of a friend from cancer.

The same day, I meet with my emergency counsellor, a last session for the calendar year. About to leave, I stand arrested in the doorway, as she recalls we haven't made a date for the next session. We'd been meeting weekly, formally and informally. I haven't realised quite how much that regular, consistent holding pattern mattered, how much I am living from one to the next, until that moment when we realise with both our upcoming holidays away, it will be six more weeks till the next one. And if that feels hard enough, there is also a planned time away for her of many weeks, in just a few months' time.

In shock, distressed, with way too long to go till I see a therapist again, the inevitable happens. Suicidal thoughts begin again, and this time, I feet horribly alone, and deeply ashamed. I feel like a helpless child, dependent, clingy, scared.

I need to find some other help. At least to practise. To get at least a little more sorted, a little less desperate, before my counsellor becomes totally unavailable.

I make my first contact with a helpline the day after Boxing Day, a public holiday.

Holiday time is often stressful in families, but for me, it should not have been. I had almost no responsibility at all for our family

Christmas celebrations this time — a few presents to purchase from me, a real tree to buy. Our four grown-up offspring — all home together for the first time in years — and extended family do everything else. I even managed to take part in a new tradition, a Christmas one-shot Dungeons & Dragons session. In this alternate universe, we defeat the Grinch and save Christmas.

But my husband is yet to work out how to be supportive, and I am yet to fully understand what is going on. Things are often tense. I can be angry, sullen, withdrawn, like a wounded animal: all I really know is that I'm still hurting like hell, and I don't know where to get help to get me through the coming weeks. It's a while before I realise why it hurts so much that all our offspring are so happy to be home with us.

There are thirty to forty helplines in New Zealand. Most of them require you to ring and use your voice. Some are for youth, some for specific needs. I'm not young enough or old enough, not in a minority group, not rainbow, not having problems with alcohol or just depression or partner violence. And to complicate matters even more, I feel I need to text, not ring: when I am in enough agony to need help, my ability to talk shuts down, to anyone. There is no way I feel I could make a phone call. All this narrows the options down to two.

1.06 pm, on the day after Christmas Day, I text.

'Hi. This is my first time using this helpline. I have over a month to wait until my next therapist appointment which is going to be tough.'

I wait.

Eight minutes later, an automated text back comes through.

'Welcome to Lifeline. We will be with you as soon as possible but could take some time due to high demand. If you can't wait, please contact 1737 or call 111.'

Twenty-one minutes later, I text back.

'Don't bother will try again another day.' I'm bemused. This is a helpline, isn't it?

Eighty-six minutes after my initial text comes their reply.

'Hello, this is Andrea from Lifeline, we apologies [their spelling] for the delay. I hear we are going through a tough time right now. I am available if you still need support?'

Do they not know how to read? I think. I'm grumpy now and in no mood to even text.

I know I'm not in actual immediate danger, which puts me well down the priority list for any support. But this is a crisis helpline, isn't it? Where else do I go? Waiting an hour and a half just seems... ridiculous.

Another seven minutes go by.

'Hello, I am just checking in, are you still there with me?'

'Hello, I am aware you haven't responded back to my text messages, I am just checking in again. Do you still need support from us?'

'It seems like you might be busy right now, I will have to end the conversation here. We appreciate you for reaching out for support that takes courage to do. We are here if you ever need us again. take care.'

A few days later, New Year's Day, I try again. This time to the other helpline that accepts texts, 1737.

10.28 am.

'Struggling with feeling suicidal', I tap out the text.

My expectations of help aren't high.

The automated reply comes back quickly, only five minutes this time, and it is much more lengthy, friendly, and somewhat helpful.

'Kia ora, awesome that you've reached out to 1737. We're here to support you! ...'

It goes on to explain that there may be a delay, to ring 111 if it's an emergency, or to contact your local mental health crisis assessment team for mental health crisis support.

'... Have a think about what you're here to talk about — is it to talk and be heard, or needing advice and tips, or are you unsure?'

I find the suggestion to think what I am there for, while waiting, to be a useful one. Even if it is hard to do when distressed. It seems practical and realistic. But the onus, as always, feels like it is on me the caller to decide how much of a crisis I'm actually in. The layers of possible help seem confusing. I'm not about to jump, so not 111. That's easy. But who is the crisis assessment team? Do I need them for 'just' daily suicidal thoughts, that sometimes go away for a week or two? But that has been going on now for nearly three months.

Is that *enough* of a crisis? How bad am I, really?

That's what I'm calling them for, to get help finding out! Why does it feel so complicated?

11.21 am.

The helpline responds. It's nearly fifty minutes after I got their automated message. This doesn't jar quite as much, given the last helpline's wait time had been nearly ninety minutes. But it does feel a little off.

'Kia ora you've reached Amy at Need to Talk. I can see you are having thoughts of hurting yourself. Before we talk further, can you please share with me your name and any other ways you identify??'

I hesitate. Do I even want to share my name? This feels like a trick question before we've even got started. My trust is low. I somehow summon up courage to reply.

'I'm Robyn.'

From there, this skilled counsellor manages to get my key concern out, discuss, and then asks after half an hour of our back-and-forth texts, 'How are your energy levels today?'

With a jolt I come back to reality. It's nearly midday and I'm still in bed. Even in my low states of late, that's unusual. We discuss how I could be motivated to get up and stay up: I say I'll try: I ask whether if I make contact again, I'll need to start all over again with explanations. She responds that she does write up notes, that I can ask the next person to review those, but usually each call is treated from scratch. That feels hugely frustrating, but I thank her, sincerely. Our exchange ends at 12.05 pm.

January 11th. I make contact again, concerned that now I've done some research into suicide methods. It's 6.36 am. But this time there's no quick automatic text reply.

I wait, puzzled. It's not even a public holiday this time.

At 7.30 am I get a text from them but via another number.

'Kia ora, thank [their spelling] for reaching out to the Need to Talk We are very sorry but due to technical issues we are unable to provide timely support at the moment. If this is an emergency or you're feeling unsafe, please call 111 for immediate assistance or if you are experiencing a mental health crisis, please contact your local crisis team.'

WTF? Now what?

I decide to risk trying the other text-able helpline again, despite their dire wait time on my first attempt.

I start a text conversation with helpline number two.

Meanwhile at 12.34 pm, six hours after making contact, a reply comes from the first one.

'Kia ora, this is Bea, thanks for reaching out to the Need to Talk Helpline, just so I can support you better can you please tell me your name, age, gender, ethnicity and whereabouts you are based in NZ? Thanks.'

Then another:

'I apologise for the delay — we're having a higher than usual volume of calls/txts at the moment — thank you for your patience'.

I'm so, so angry, and confused, and disappointed.

'I'm having a conversation with another helpline right now,' I reply.

With nothing riding on this contact, I feel assertive enough to provide some feedback.

'That's also a truckload of questions to ask someone at once, why not just start with just a name? [smiley face emoji]'

This is the reality check of helpline support. I get, invariably, a different person every time, with a different approach. While it's difficult to work round this, it's about the worst possible way to support someone with trauma. But I figure anyone in mental distress of any kind will surely baulk at such a long list of questions all at once. Immediately you are reduced to a set of data, not a person — the exact opposite of what they're presumably trying to achieve. Only bureaucracy treats you this way, not anyone trying to establish a relationship. And in the helpline business, I would think that establishing a relationship, however fleeting, could be life or death.

Meantime, at 11.48 am, after waiting five hours, I contact Lifeline.

'Is someone available to answer a question about ideation and level of risk?' I text.

I receive the now expected brief autoreply, then at 12.22 pm, a real reply. So just thirty-four minutes' wait time.

A useful exchange happens. At one point, I say I don't really fit the high-risk category of young, male, and friendless. The counsellor texts back that feeling suicidal because of trauma is 'more common still than we often talk about across many demographics'. She strongly encourages me to keep reaching out when I need to, 'so that we can explore some coping mechanisms in the moment and support you in general with what you are going through'.

I have to break off the conversation, because given how long I've been waiting, I'm now out and about buying lunch with my daughter. We're on holiday, which makes everything harder: more decisions, stress, lack of any normal routine, visiting family and friends who haven't been told much about how I am. My husband is upset and has gone off by himself for an hour. I've only just started to tell our own grown-up kids about the suicidal thoughts. I'm running out of energy.

Another day, in distress, another call.

3.13 pm 18 January, to Lifeline:

'I'm struggling with how painful I feel today. No ideation yet but it would almost be better than feeling like this.'

The reply — after the automated one — comes a record seven minutes later. Speed record. But this text conversation rapidly starts to deteriorate for me; the same old questions are asked, I refer them back to the helpline notes from last time, and the tone is just off enough that I'm irked.

'This is not helping much. I'm just repeating things I've already said and getting annoyed. I'll try another time if needed.'

'I understand. Before you go, can I please check if you are going to be safe today?'

Shit, I think.

No rapport has been built, no trust established, I've said they're not being helpful but said nothing to make someone question my safety. I've not had this asked before. It's blunt and lands very badly.

I'm furious but want to see what the response will be.

'Just out of curiosity what would you do when someone answers no to that question??!'

'I would need to put a safety plan in place. That can involve support from your family or friends. If need be, it would involve a welfare check from the Police as they can do these and are 24/7 service. Your safety is important to us, can I please check before you go, do you have a plan for suicide?'

A welfare check from the Police, if I don't answer right? Jeez. What on earth does she think I'll reply to that one?

'No plan today.'

The counsellor/volunteer texts 'thanks' and suggests trying

different distraction strategies from those I've tried before (both unspecified).

'If you feel like brainstorming self-care strategies at any time, or anything changes and you feel unsafe — at risk of taking action on suicidal thoughts, can we agree for you to phone us or text again?'

I reply, testily, 'I will contact *someone* when needed [emphasis in my head].'

That seems to be enough to stave off an unnecessary visit from the police, and the conversation is closed off. I feel like I've had the ultimate tick-the-box conversation. There's been not one second of human connection here.

It's now off-putting to have that interchange potentially on my notes for this helpline. It feels over the top and unnecessary and clunky. I feel threatened, not supported, not seen.

Two weeks later, I try once more, to the other helpline. This is my sixth try at reaching out to helplines. I think.

It's 9.49 am, 31 January 2023.

'Struggling with suicidal ideation... Again'.

At 10.23 am a counsellor/volunteer texts back. A thirty-four-minute wait again. Could be worse.

She starts with an apology for the delay.

'My name is Brenda, before we continue may I ask your name, age, ethnicity, gender, and where you are in New Zealand? This can help me support you better and is completely optional.'

I miss seeing the 'optional' bit, in my distress, and see red.

A discussion happens about whether she can see any of my previous notes: I explain my struggle with being asked a whole list of questions at once.

'It just triggers frustration and anger and wrecks my ability to go further in the conversation with you. I'm going to finish up this conversation here because of this. You're better off dealing with someone else since you're so busy.'

'… please be aware that this free helpline is for brief support only and a different counsellor will answer each time, and we are required to ask demographics at the beginning of each session, as we can never assume we are talking to the same person each time. Hope that makes sense.'

I'm so, so over this kind of 'support'. I do not reply.

The helpline worker possibly recognises from this silence that their tone was less than helpful.

'You are welcome to contact us again anytime, we are available 24/7. If you are at imminent risk, please contact your local mental health crisis team or emergency services on 111. Take care.'

A newspaper article from a couple of years ago pops up in my searches around this time. It's one of those feel-goods about a young man who'd been on the brink of suicide a couple of years back but now was running an Ironman. Turns out, when he texted the helpline 1737 for the first time, he got a *phone call* back *within two minutes*. From a counsellor who stayed on the line for *two hours* talking him out of making an attempt, and actually being helpful.

All he'd texted was, 'I need help.'

I try to be glad for him and fail. I'm just insanely jealous. That's the photo perfect story, the young man saved by the timely helpline assistance, now look at him go.

'What about me?' screams in my head.

Ironman? Most days it's hard enough to move from the bedroom to bathroom to living room.

The helpline staff are trying, I can tell. Some — a small minority — of the counsellors or volunteers are genuinely helpful for me. But the system and their training, as I've experienced in most of my interactions, are not set up to help those who need a consistent, trauma-informed approach. And as I am to find out, neither is the much-mentioned local crisis team. Nor most GPs. Nor, even, many therapists.

CALLING 111

*'Complex trauma isn't about imperfect parenting.
Every parent is imperfect.
Every childhood is imperfect.
Complex trauma is about a toxic blend of you-suck, you-don't-matter, you-can't-escape, & here-are-some-WAY-developmentally-inappropriate-experiences-to-cope-with.'*

— Dr Glenn Patrick Doyle: Instagram,
23 November 2023, @drdoylesays

I went to primary school on Auckland's North Shore, in the 70s. The Shore was mostly affluent already, but not yet to the dizzying heights it would become. I had a mix of friends, some from families my mother would have defined as working class, some with fathers in the professions.

I arrived at school there aged six. Almost everyone else started at five, but I had started school in Jamaica, in the English system, aged four and a half. I could read two years above my age. My mother said the school had wanted to put me in the class for that level, but she'd said no, it would be socially too hard. There were no gifted programmes in my childhood. The only answer was skipping a year, or two. I skipped one, therefore fitting in to neither my year group nor my ability group.

I had music lessons, got taken to netball and tennis, got orthodontic braces, glasses then contact lenses, lots of good food, even Cordon Bleu. Mother was a very good cook. What I didn't have was a feeling of safety, closeness, or love; I don't recall being hugged, or wanting to hug, I have no memory of being read to or asked how I felt (by anybody — even when suicide was an issue for my sibling). I listen to a therapist on YouTube call this kind of childhood the sort that is 'good on paper'. I have no memory of ever wanting to be in my mother's company — as an adult, my husband had to insist we went every other year to my mother's for Christmas. I never wanted to go.

At some point we must have had a lesson at school on what to do in emergencies, such as when is the correct time to phone for help. It was most likely an attempt to stop nuisance calls to the national emergency 111 line from bored school children.

I called 111 when I was nine, and not from boredom.

My oldest sister, Liz, was in the hallway of our home. She'd come back from England to live with us again, I don't really know why. That evening she was gasping, struggling for breath, grabbing at the phone, snatching it off its cradle. The rotary dial phone, hardwired to the wall, sat on the telephone-table-with-seat in the hallway. It was a darkish olive-green regulation landline phone, because this was the 70s, and there was little choice in New Zealand as to phone colour. I think you could get cream. Or maybe black. That was about it.

I don't recall ever seeing my sister like this before. Her distress, her panic, is still vivid in my mind over four decades later.

I don't remember making the call, but I know it was me who did. I can see myself, standing at the front door. It's open, and the light is fading as the summer evening comes. I wear a pale blue T-shirt with white and navy stripes across the yoke, and pyjama shorts. I must have been getting ready for bed when I heard Liz's panicked breathing.

I stand, desperately waiting, half turned to the inside, trying to reassure my sister that help is coming. The ambulance arrives and comes down our awkwardly steep driveway without any seeming concern. The officers come inside. By this time my sister's breathing has calmed down. One officer notices the phone dangling off the hook, replaces it, then with dawning comprehension looks around and at me and asks, 'Who made the call?'

That's where my memory blanks out, with someone noticing me. I have no memory of anything said after that, or any discussion with me by my family at all, that evening or later. I remember the officers explaining to Liz that she had experienced an asthma attack, that she could use a paper bag over her mouth and nose next time, that she should go to the doctor for medication. Perhaps she did, as I don't remember seeing her have breathing issues again while I lived with her.

I do remember very clearly that the other person in the house that evening, the other grown-up, was our mother. Dad must have been out at choir practice, or a church vestry meeting, or something. He wasn't around. Our mother sat at the far end of our large living room watching TV. The living room door was open. She could see and hear her eldest daughter unable to breathe and needing help. She could see and hear me making a call to 111. She didn't get up. She may have got up to come talk to the officers when they arrived. I don't remember that part so well, but I think that is when she did come to the hallway.

I learned that day that something life-threatening could be happening and our mother wouldn't move to help in any way. It confirmed what all my siblings had known, what one of them said to me only recently, now, in my fifties. What I only now can verbalise to myself, to my therapist, to my husband.

'We never went to Mum when we were hurt,' my sister told me in one of our post-election loss chats. 'We went to Dad.'

Which would be not so bad, except that from the time I was six until my parents moved me out at sixteen, most of my dad's time and energy at home was spent in trying to look after my sister Tina, in and out of psychiatric wards. While also being the sole breadwinner. Because, as my mother loudly and proudly announced to someone in my hearing one day in my primary school years, she'd told my dad before they'd got married not to expect her to 'look after anyone sick'. She said she was 'no good' at it.

On one occasion in the turmoil of Tina's coming and going from the psych ward, I remember our mother declaring loudly to someone: 'Of course I want Tina home. I just don't want her illness.'

Even as an under-ten-year-old, that comment felt weird.

How can you separate a person from their unwellness? Does a parent get to choose?

The unspoken, or at times even spoken, message from our mother was — don't expect help when sick or hurt, don't be a nuisance, don't do or say anything to bring her shame or burst her toxically, sickening romantic expectations of a rosy life; don't expect support.

Mother talked loudly and often about how stressful it was to deal with Tina's illness. For years I accepted the easier reality that the stress and tension in the house was due to this 'illness' of my sister. I had some sympathy for our mother; I could see it would be stressful. I blinded myself despite the evidence, unable to acknowledge fully what I had seen unconsciously — that it was my mother's presence which was far, far more stressful and toxic than anyone else in the household: that it was her presence, in truth, which was instrumental in bringing about our distress and much of our unwellness.

When I was thirteen or fourteen, my mother took me on a house visit to two families. One was our neighbours, in the adjoining unit, a dozen steps down our shared driveway. Two older women. The other was to a husband and wife, both teachers at schools I was in or had been in, one had taught me just a year or two previously. This one, the wife, looked at me oddly. Because why should I be there? These were condolence visits to families who had lost an adult child — to suicide. I still shake my head over this. I wouldn't take my young teens on such a visit. I would talk about it with them, yes. Not take on visits. What good would it do to those grieving?

And now it dawns on me: I was a shield. If I was there, a young teen, the mourners would show only an appropriate amount of emotion. They wouldn't go into details. Mother could look good by doing her duty but not have to sit with anyone's grief.

WILL IT WORK?

'Being emotionally unaffected by an upsetting event isn't strength or resilience. It is dissociation.'

— Cecile Tucker: Instagram, 26 March 2024, @ceciletuckercounselling

In February, four months post-election, I started with the EMDR provider I'd seen in mid-December.

At least, I was meant to.

I'd been waiting for seven long, long weeks. We'd agreed, back in that first session in mid-December, that having only one further appointment before Christmas and the holiday break would not work. The therapist was unavailable the whole school holidays, six weeks. Her parting, very matter-of-fact comment was that I could expect suicidal thoughts to return, and that when they did, I should simply 'welcome the thoughts for the helpful protective mechanism that they are but tell them you aren't going to act on them'.

It took months to fully digest that comment.

At first, I thought this was incredibly wise and useful — until the thoughts returned. The ability to welcome anything when I feel this distressed is very low. I struggle to welcome these intruders, this evidence of my inability to function like a 'normal' human being. It takes time to work this aphorism into practice. Even then, it still feels deficient as a supportive tool. I am, however, grateful that the therapist wasn't anxious or upset about me having these thoughts. That she had something, anything, useful to say about them.

She also promised me she'd write up notes from this first session, and email them to me before our second session, in February. I didn't ask for or expect this; it was her offer.

But with all the tension of the summer so far, the terrible experiences trying to get helpline support, my hypervigilant mind is now in overdrive, looking constantly for danger, for incompetence or lack of consistency in those I reach out to. I am terrified of anything getting worse, but the fear itself makes everything worse: it feels like a death spiral.

A week before my February appointment, I realise the promised email has not arrived.

I email a polite query, in case she's forgotten or her email to me has gone astray.

And then I wait.

Six days later, with my much longed-for, much-needed appointment meant to be the next day, there is still no email. I launch into full panic mode over this uncertainty.

What has happened? Where is she? Why won't she answer?

In deep distress, that afternoon I text her.

And still, silence.

The next morning, in business hours with just an hour before my appointment is due, my fear and frustration boil over into anger. I text again.

'Given you haven't bothered to reply to either text or email, I assume my appointment today to be cancelled. It was unlikely to be of benefit given I've hardly been able to speak this week and am exhausted.'

The reply comes within minutes, a profuse apology, a reference to an emergency. And then, she refers me to a couple of websites — to look for a new therapist. I thought I'd just had one appointment cancelled, not my ability to have any further appointments with her at all. I am shell-shocked. Her text seems very optimistic about my chances of finding another therapist. I struggle to share her positivity.

On the recommendation of a friend, I try emailing a psychologist. That email gets no reply.

I try one EMDR therapist listed on a website with no luck but am given the name of another. This time, I am lucky — an appointment for next week. But she can't give me a regular time slot, as these are all full. No problem, I think, I'm not working. Or studying. Or volunteering, or — anything.

The first session passes as expected, giving a brief history of why I'm here, checking whether EMDR is a good option for me. I cling to the fact I *am* here, that treatment can finally begin. We discuss early on whether I might consider antidepressants for my depressive symptoms; she tells me this won't interfere with EMDR, that some people need that stabilising influence of medication to be able to tackle this therapy. I ask for a letter to my GP. It clearly states I am being treated for trauma but may fit the criteria for depression — necessary if I am to get antidepressants.

Several GP visits follow. What I want, what I ask for, is oversight: some health professional other than the EMDR provider to check in with, to see how I was going. I had decided not to try antidepressants after all, and I tell the GP so on my first visit. I have a gut feeling this isn't for me. I had a short history some years ago of unhelpful reactions to such meds, and this is even on my medical records (rather oddly, under the heading 'Allergies').

But at the second GP visit, several weeks after the first, the doctor doggedly goes back to it. Explain quite why I didn't want antidepressants, comes the firm request.

I do, as best I can. The doctor seems unconvinced.

I ask what else is on offer. I'm told there is a free thirty-minute session with a health worker I can take up. I stare in uncomprehending disbelief.

'You really think one half-hour session is going to help when you've already diagnosed moderate to severe depression last time?'

'Just explaining what's available' is the defensive reply. There's no explanation that I could have more than one appointment with the health worker, as I discover later. But this service is intended for only mild to moderate mental health issues, and this GP had clearly put me in the moderate to severe category last time.

I'm then told the other option is a referral to the community mental health team. The crisis team. The doctor hesitates, their face guarded, edgy.

'They will almost certainly want to talk about medication with you.'

I'm being the difficult patient, the one who won't tick the box and won't accept the 'right' help.

Anything else at all, I'm told, I need to source myself, privately. The problem is, I already *am* doing that — and once a week is not enough support just now. Therapists do not provide an on-call service or check-ins in between appointments. That's not how therapy works. I feel stuck.

NEVER A PROBLEM

'A well-behaved child isn't always an emotionally well child. And an emotionally well child isn't always well-behaved.'

— Eli Harwood: Instagram, 6 February 2024, @attachmentnerd

In my last year at high school students were allowed to wear 'mufti', regular clothes, instead of the school uniform. This seventh-form year (now called Year 13) was still relatively small; in a school like mine with about 1200 to 1500 students over five year-levels, only about seventy of us stayed on for the last year.

One day I decided to experiment. I had a black sleeveless jumpsuit which I paired with a white shirt, black sleeveless woollen vest, and my dad's crimson velvet bow tie he wore for the North Shore Male Voice Choir.

He sang tenor. I can remember him still, practising the 'Slaves Chorus' around the house: 'Speed your journey... my thoughts and my longings....', an aching, yearning song the context of which I had no idea. My mother sometimes taped the choir's performances on a portable cassette deck. In a copy I had later converted to a digital file, I can almost imagine I hear his voice still, singing that chorus.

It was the first term of our three-term school year. Back then, the seventh form was the most important year for anyone going to university. You could get university entrance the year before, but by doing another year, you could gain an A or B Bursary which came with a hundred dollars or so a year for your undergraduate degree, or the coveted, mystical Junior Scholarship, awarded to only two per cent of students. My school counted themselves lucky if just one student a year achieved this crowning glory. The best schools in Auckland would manage several each year, with intensive extra tuition.

I walked out the door. My mother was sitting on the telephone table seat, on the phone. She began praising me to her listener — probably my godmother, the only friend of my mother's who seemed to spend any time with her.

She described my clothes appreciatively. She didn't pause her call to talk to me directly. She then said something like, 'Robyn's never a problem. I could send her round the world by herself, she's so capable!'

It sounds like a great compliment. But I reeled inside for a moment. I was only sixteen. I could get myself to school, or badminton, or other activities in our area. But I'd never so much as left town by myself. I was in an instant filled with fear, so overwhelming that I shut it down, focused on getting to school.

I didn't ever wear that outfit again, or anything so daringly different that might catch attention, despite no-one at school making any negative remarks on it. I didn't make the connection until forty years later: my mother was justifying herself for the choice they had just made. Soon after they sold our North Shore house at the end of the first school term and moved up the coast to a popular retirement spot near lots of beaches. They did organise for me to live with my oldest sister Liz, who owned a small old two-bedroom house on another part of the Shore — further away from my school, so now I had to bus instead of walk or cycle.

My mother wasn't about to send me around the world. But she was getting rid of me, offloading me so that she could be nearer her beloved beaches, foisting me onto my sister for two-thirds of the most important year of high school. I did have food, and my sister was there at evenings and weekends. But Liz worked full time and had no energy to support me emotionally after her working day. It was another five years or more before she finally received her diagnosis of multiple sclerosis. We were not particularly close: Liz had left home for England from Jamaica when I was about four, even before our sister June left. Liz returned and lived in our parents' home for a few years before buying her own place. She had their financial support as banks would not give enough mortgage money in the early 80s to a single woman. She was very quiet, reserved, frugal, anxious, and her poor relationship with our mother was blamed openly by our mother on her birth — apparently induced by cod liver oil — and the rigid four-hourly feeding schedules of the time. Any reason, except herself.

I worked very, very hard that year at my studies. It was the loneliest year of my life. I don't recall phoning my parents, or them phoning me to check on how I was going. I remember our dad joking to Liz about the number of extra milk bottles she'd need to put out by the road, because I drank 'so much milk'. There was food money paid to Liz, there was a clothing allowance paid to me. There was zero discussion about what I wanted, or other kinds of support most sixteen-year-olds need. I was just expected to not be a problem, and to get on with it, fitting around my parents' needs, not mine.

IT'S MENTAL

In those early post-election months, I am repeatedly struck by just how physical it feels, to have a 'mental' illness.

I catch myself heaving deep, deep sighs, at random, a kind of sigh I do not recall ever experiencing or noticing in anyone else. I'm mystified, until I watch a TV series recommended to me for its portrayal of grief. It's called *After Life*. The first series is R18 for its suicide attempt scenes, going down a notch from series two and three to R16 — I assume for the near constant swearing of the main character, Tony, a man in midlife who loses his beloved wife to cancer. Tony sighs like me. I still remember the feeling of seeing it for the first time, on the screen of my tablet, shouting to the empty lounge, 'That's it! That's what I do!' I watch all three seasons within a few weeks and then feel bereft, like I've lost a good friend. This portrayal of deep grief and suicidality speaks on a level no-one around me seems able to do. And the swearing feels essential. Despite a childhood of the strictest non-swearing kind — 'bum' was an unusable swear word to my mother, as was the exclamation 'Oh my God!' for which she humiliated me in front of another adult for my ignorance in using such a terribly sinful phrase.

In the months that follow, my use of swearing escalates noticeably. Especially 'what the fuck'. Life seems to become just a series of WTF moments, I tell a friend. I buy myself a suitable mug with WTF prominent.* It arrives, with a clearly lopsided print. A replacement is sent when I point this out. Not even a WTF mug is done right, but at least the mistake is speedily sorted.

In just a few months — with no obvious change in diet or exercise — I gain over ten per cent of my body weight, mostly sitting around my midriff. A therapist nods at this information.

'Stress hormones will do that,' she says. There is no judgement.

It feels somehow humiliating, though, having to go out and buy new jeans, and send winter coats that no longer fit to the op shop. My body is telling the world there's something wrong with me. I'm not in good shape. I'm a less-than-normal being. Around me I see suburban women in their forties and fifties losing weight, going to gym, doing protein diets; older women doing long walks and physically demanding volunteer roles.

And the exhaustion, beyond words, beyond anything I've experienced even as a full-time mother of four. Months, and months, and months of exhaustion.

My husband tries to encourage me to go out for a walk with him. Just our usual short ramble around local streets, nothing demanding. I agree without wanting to. I feel obliged to at least try. Health professionals constantly hold up exercising and moving your body as good for you. But it is no magic pill, and I feel no better after such walks. Those days when I am so, so painfully sluggish, so unable to achieve anything like a normal walking pace, unable to force my resisting body, feeling disgust and frustration no matter how much patience my husband shows. I learn to wait until I feel a

---

* 'The Naked Pastor' created a cartoon called 'The Most Sincere Prayer', where a cartoon stick figure is praying by his bed: 'Dear Lord… WTF?', available on mugs or prints. I get no commission.

spurt of wanting to be active. I do not want to force my body. It feels violating, somehow.

Almost unconsciously I turn to breathing techniques learned from my first midwife, when the trigger is too strong, the flashbacks too intense, when I feel my very breath stopping and I need to remind myself simply to breathe. My mind goes back to that first long night of labour. I went through four births without an epidural. This feels worse, because this kind of labour, this trauma response, seems to have no end.

'I can't handle being "in labour" for the rest of my life!' I complain to a friend.

My gut often feels bloated. My middle is a balloon stretched to its limits, unable to pop, like that terrible aunt who is blown up in the third Harry Potter book. Unlike her, this bloating does not lighten my being, but weighs me down, heavy and forbidding. My brain feels fuzzy, physically fuzzy. I'm unable to concentrate, reading is difficult, decision-making feels like a joke.

Then comes the twitching. I notice that my arm or leg muscles will simply twitch out of nowhere. It takes a while to realise that these often signal that I've been triggered that day or the day before. My body is trying to shake out the tension like a wild animal newly escaped from a predator: twitching that continues off and on into my second year post-election.

My muscles get tense, even when I've just woken up.

I've had tinnitus for as long as I can remember. I look that up one day on my phone, and sure enough, researchers have linked this to trauma too.

Someone in an online support group asks, 'What are the tell-tale signs of C-PTSD? I realise that people with ptsd are most likely light sleepers and could recognise family members or friends by the sound of their footfalls...' — ohhhhhh. You too?

Direct eye contact becomes extraordinarily difficult, threatening. Especially in a therapy room. I become aware of how much I avoid eye contact. My neurodiverse family members empathise. 'That's what happens. We get sensory overload, Mum.' It's not the first or last time I see strange similarities between my trauma response and autism. Different causes, some same symptoms: our nervous system overloaded, we respond in noticeably similar ways.

Over a year post-election, I start doing an exercise session by video call with one of my grown daughters. It is simple stretching, very light weights. My body feels tangled and stuck and hopeless. We laugh a lot. I often have to think about which arm I've just moved, and which is the other one to swap to for the stretch we're doing. One side of my body is noticeably less able in almost all the exercises.

My daughter is patient, encouraging, understanding beyond her years, dealing with her own health issues that make regular exercise a necessity. I cannot sit cross-legged, touch my toes, or hold basic core muscle positions for long. I must think hard before starting a star-jump — there is no instinctive recognition of how that movement of my body through space will happen. In some ways, my body is lost to me.*

I am deeply, deeply grateful to my offspring. There is no way I am ready to go to a gym class, to deal with strangers, to see the looks in the eyes of those for whom such sessions would be mere warm-ups to the real deal. And anyway, paying for a personal trainer when I am already doing psychotherapy at $180 a week feels like a luxury.

On a visit to my GP, I discover that I have white coat syndrome. The first blood pressure measurement comes out high: I don't see the numbers, but the doctor asks to try again. They try three more times over the next five or ten minutes in my double appointment.

The GP hands me the pink Post-it note with the readings.

151/103
147/98

---

* Chapter 6, *The Body Keeps the Score*: 'Losing Your Body, Losing Your Self'.

133/96

133/86

We discuss this, briefly. White coat syndrome isn't mentioned; I look that up at home myself. My GP then proceeds to give a cut-and-paste lecture on making lifestyle changes. I sit barely taking it in, surprised, because no lifestyle change happened during this appointment, and here is the proof in my hand that something else is driving down my blood pressure from unacceptably high, to reasonably fine. They suggest I get my own blood pressure monitor for home use.

The first reading I get at home is low enough to make me think I've bought a dud. It's four days after the GP visit, with no 'lifestyle changes' at all. The reading is 115/79.

I play with the blood pressure monitor for some weeks, before leaving it aside in the cupboard. The readings aren't always low. High readings happen some days — days when I realise I have been noticeably triggered. A friend jokes that if I had a permanent monitoring set-up, I could tell which people I find the most triggering, just by looking at the readings. I don't need it. By now, I've had enough triggered episodes to be fairly sure of who, why, and when. Things that come as a surprise or shock, people who I need to help me being incompetent, me feeling incompetent, inconsistent interactions, unclear boundaries, me feeling unseen — being treated as a number, a diagnostic category, filling in forms, or receiving generic copy-and-paste information. All elements of a modern civilised society.

IT'S HORMONAL

My youngest of four children was born the year I turned thirty-five. It's a family joke that we chose to have another child because the last one I'd found easy — even with three children under the age of three and a half. It had been 'easy', because for the first time, the process of weaning off breastfeeding hadn't caused my world to spiral.

Around the eight-month mark after birth, weaning my first babies onto solids, my cycle started back. And along with that, a vicious suite of hormonal symptoms that my doctor routinely put down to depression and attempted to say was depression and, therefore, that I needed antidepressants. I was exhausted, even though we sleep-trained our kids from an early age and got embarrassingly good amounts of sleep: I had a near-constant 'yuck' feeling of nausea/bloating around my abdomen. I had mood swings, low mood, fuzzy-headedness, even the occasional flicker of suicidal thoughts. This wasn't regular 'baby blues', it wasn't until months and months after birth.

Each time I got pregnant, all these symptoms went away. My

doctor never asked me about this in his history-taking, and I didn't make the connection.

But none of this happened after our third child was born. I was astounded how much better life felt, how much more capable I was. We took a bit longer to get pregnant with our fourth, but along she came.

And then, five months in, I'd had enough. My mood was plummeting already. I woke up one morning in tears, knowing I just couldn't face breastfeeding any more, and no-one had shown me how to mix bottle feeding with breastfeeding. I called out for help to our church family. They rallied magnificently. We spent a day with devoted women holding and caring for my baby, trying to get her to take the bottle, while others kept me company, fed me, and made sure I was okay.

If possible, I wouldn't recommend instant weaning. It takes days for the breasts to get the message; they are overfull, heavy, achy reminders of what felt like failure. Baby took half a day, before hunger got the better of her and she accepted a bottle of formula. But the symptoms persisted for months, and darkness descended on me.

I got desperate enough to try a brief course of antidepressants. I couldn't handle the side-effects — nausea was a symptom I wanted to be rid of, not endure from medication. I was worried about the small-print side-effects: the increased risk of suicide. My doctor, obviously nervous, suggested another type. I read the small print, then read him the riot act. I had asked for my iron levels to be checked, not for more medication. He hadn't listened. My trust in him was lost, and we parted ways not long after.

Somehow by chance, a woman from church mentioned an alternative clinic, who used bio-identical progesterone as part of their treatment. I'd never heard of it. I was sceptical, but desperate. My youngest was a year old, my eldest just about eight, and I needed to be there for them. The nurse's assessment and history-taking were far more thorough than anything I'd ever experienced in the regular health system. She also got me to do a saliva test for progesterone levels. To this day, not even normal menopause clinics will do this, let alone most doctors.

This was the early 2000s, when bio-identical progesterone was berated as 'snake oil', and controversy around hormones centred on hormone replacement therapy for perimenopausal women. Yet in my late thirties, my doctor simply hadn't thought of the possibility that my hormones were involved in my symptoms, or why, or how to sort the issue. In the Western corporatised bio-medical model of 'health', pills are almost always the answer.

My progesterone level was stunningly low.

I was told to rub a specific number of drops of progesterone oil on specific parts of the body, for the first twenty-one days of my cycle. I was told I would feel the difference in two months. I was doubtful, but dutiful. I could see no alternative.

Two months later, it was like a miraculous return to my normal self. My facial expression so radically changed, everyone commented on it. Despite having four children under the age of eight, my energy, motivation, and joy in life returned. It was transformational, and I stayed using the oil for five years, until the clinic's out-of-town service and friendly GP finished up. A doctor was necessary to prescribe the progesterone, but most doctors still thought it was alternative nonsense.

I thought I didn't need it anymore, so I stopped.

Four years later, I was back at my new doctor with nausea.

'Irritable Bowel Syndrome' was the suggestion. I was sent to a specialist.

I spent $300 or $350 for fifteen minutes' consultation. Quite a few minutes of that was listening to him describe his symptoms, what it felt like anytime he forgot and ate a pear. He asked very few questions, assumed the diagnosis was correct, and gave offhand advice about a FODMAP diet. None of this seemed right. My symptoms didn't quite match. I felt dimly, somehow, unseen.

Another four years went by. Symptoms increased, not hugely,

but enough to alarm me. I remembered what it felt like to be so low. I looked around Wellington for a doctor who dealt in bio-identical hormones. There was only one, and while she did prescribe me bio-identical progesterone, over the months that followed, she showed signs of being incompetent and much, much too alternative. She 'tested' me on two consecutive visits for allergies by getting me to hold a full medicine-sized bottle of some mixture, and something else, connected, making a 'circle of energy'... From this she 'diagnosed' first that I was allergic to yeast, and next visit, that I was allergic to something quite different. Her advice on diet was perfunctory — eliminating yeast from your diet is no small feat. On the second visit, I challenged her.

'That's not what you said last time. Last time you said there was a yeast allergy!'

Did she not even take notes, I asked myself?

She harrumphed and mumbled, 'That's not how it works,' turning her head quickly away from me, staring at her computer screen, moving on to something else. I repeated my comments about feeling bloated despite taking the progesterone.

She had me lie down, for the first time, on the examination table, and pull up my shirt.

She poked and prodded my middle, then leered over me, gloating.

'It's the weight around your middle. You need to lose weight. Being overweight is causing your discomfort'.

She herself was as thin as the proverbial rake.

I was astounded. I felt humiliated. I also smelt a rat. Sure, I was maybe a couple of kilos more round the middle than I'd like, but nowhere near enough to cause physical discomfort, certainly not bloating and nausea. I checked my BMI once home: not overweight. I was disgusted and left her practice. Belatedly I looked up online reviews. I wasn't the only disgruntled customer. There had been formal complaints. She retired not long after.

Back to square one and resigned to conventional medicine, I

went to my regular doctor. Now of an age for perimenopause to be considered, I was put on Provera, a medroxyprogesterone which is similar but not identical to the body's progesterone, and an oestrogen patch. A visit to a specialised menopause clinic was strongly recommended. I did so, lucky to get in, as the waiting list skyrocketed soon after. But on describing my symptoms, which didn't include hot flushes, I was told I was unusual. Only five to ten per cent of women had my symptoms. This should have been a red flag, but as a desperate woman, I went along with the advice.

December 2021, two years after starting HRT, my husband and I were enjoying an end-of-year pantomime as a social outing for his work. There was a packed audience. It was a future imaginary Little Mermaid tale set in a watery Wellington after sea levels rise. The political references were very funny. I especially liked the character Shelley Bay. I stood up at half time, stretched, sat down. At show's end, we got up to go: and then it happened. A rush of wetness, in the half-dark I couldn't see the extent of the damage or figure out what it was. I was in shock. I got to the bathroom as quickly as possible and looked in horror in the toilet. The flood was not from my bladder. I'd lost a lot of blood, a similar amount to that lost after giving birth the third time, with similar disturbingly huge clots. Much more loss and I knew I'd faint, or worse.

I waited till most had left the toilets — it took a long time to clean up, anyway — and gingerly, slowly, went to my waiting husband.

'I need to go straight home,' I said. 'Something's happened,'

As we walked away and I clung to his arm, I explained. We got home: I made him stand outside the shower in case I fainted and wait till I'd got to the couch before he went down the road for fish and chips. I was terrified.

I had one or two more flooding incidents, not as much blood loss but always sudden and terrifying. My cycle, once unusually long, had reduced to just fourteen days — seven days of bleeding, seven days 'off'. The last flooding incident was at 4 am, the morning of surgery two months after the first flood. My back was aching.

The surgeon at the local hospital was so understanding. Before surgery, I talked about that morning's blood loss. He laughed, not in a mean way but in solidarity, and referred to *The Godfather* — not a film I'd seen but I got the reference. He suddenly got serious and looked at me steadily.

'We'll get this sorted,' he said. 'We can't have you go on like this,'

I had a D&C. A prior scan had shown a uterine fibroid, benign, likely to be causing the flooding incidents. In discussing options, I also opted for an IUD to deliver Provera more directly, in case that would help.

It was less than a year till the local body election.

Surgery or the IUD helped, with the bleeding at least. Then in January 2023, in my suicidal post-loss state, my HRT medication was changed without warning.

I open the brown bag and the container within was quite different. I now had Utrogestan, a bio-identical progesterone, instead of Provera.

Say what?

I hastily searched online and discovered that, indeed, the pharmaceutical agency Pharmac had authorised the change. I'd missed the news about this,[*] and the change had not been mentioned — as it should, for any change of prescription — by either doctor or pharmacist. Instead of Provera, there's Utrogestan. My online hunt reveals there is some evidence to show that the new formulation may even lower blood pressure.[†] No health professional has ever mentioned this hormonal connection: I quiz a

---

[*] https://www.newshub.co.nz/home/new-zealand/2022/12/new-zealand-women-now-have-free-access-to-life-changing-menopause-medication.html

[†] https://www.bloodpressureuk.org/news/news/blood-pressure-the-menopause-and-hrt.html

https://herkare.com/blog/progesterone-replacement-therapy-blood-pressure

pharmacist, and he too is unaware. Hormones, it seems, are labelled in the medical mind as a mysterious female force too erratic to be systematically measured or studied. There are precious few researchers and little to no reliable information for the layperson. It does nothing for my trauma response to feel that medically trained people who are meant to be looking after my well-being are not aware of such research and do not seem interested to learn.

So, bio-identical progesterone is now mainstream. I read the small print on my last pack of Provera. One of the side-effects is depression. I am astounded. When I challenge the menopause clinic about why I'd been put on this when I presented with low mood as one of my symptoms, they respond that I was already on HRT when I came to them... and to stop the Utrogestan if symptoms were still occurring and raise the dosage of the oestrogen patch.

In June 2023 a lightbulb moment occurred. Why not get back in touch with the 'alternative' hormone clinic? At least they understood hormones!

This time round, the clinic's nurse has even greater understanding. We talk about my trauma symptoms and my hormonal symptoms. She understands trauma. She can't guarantee that sorting out the hormone levels would end the other symptoms, but it should help. We organise the test of my progesterone levels. I mentioned the advice to stop the Utrogestan. She was horrified.

Once more, my progesterone was seriously low. For someone like me, peri or post-menopausal and taking oral micronised progesterone, the normal range according to the clinic should be between 320 and 1998 pmol/L. Mine was 185. The advice was the exact opposite of the menopause clinic — raise the progesterone dose, monitor closely, look to lower the oestrogen dose.

Progesterone is like the grandmother of the hormone system. It aids in the production of other hormones, including stress hormones. It affects mood, a range of bodily functions, things easily mistaken for IBS or depression or other misdiagnoses. It slowly dawned on me that I may not, as feared, simply have inherited the worst hormonal system ever. Instead, the bigger picture became clear. Childhood trauma had most likely impacted my progesterone levels, with too long spent on creating stress hormones. I'd spent years worried my offspring would 'inherit' the same bad deal as me. Now, I realised, it was nowhere near that simple.

It took months of increased dose to raise the levels to not just in range but upper mid-range, the nurse's goal for me, and where the bloating and fuzziness and low mood reduced a lot. Nine months and several tests later, my progesterone was a respectable 1350 pmol/L. I was still struggling with the aftermath of a year of dealing with the health system, and only a few months into psychotherapy. But at least I wasn't now also fighting a horribly imbalanced hormone system.

The nurse apologises for the cost of consultation and gives options to have them less frequently. I laugh down the phone.

'I'm in therapy at $180 a week, probably for years. Your fee is a drop in the bucket.'

Yet again it strikes me how abysmal the regular medical system is at listening to women, understanding the holistic impact of hormone levels, of trauma, of medication side-effects, and of providing financially accessible help. At some point during a gynaecological check-up, I get the Mirena removed. I most certainly don't want Provera in my system anymore.

The clinic nurse says: 'Robyn, your energy is like gold. It's so precious to you when you're so exhausted. Only spend it on those things you like doing.' The warmth and concern and wisdom is deeply appreciated.

TEARS

'Trauma is when we are not seen and known.'

— Dr Gabor Maté quoting Dr Bessel van der Kolk:
'The Myth of Normal: Trauma, Illness, and Healing in a Toxic Culture'

It took four months of EMDR therapy to get to a memory that made me cry.

I don't cry readily, almost never in front of anyone. 'Private tears', one therapist calls them.

I don't remember crying much as a child, and when I did, the response was not good.

Piano lessons were important to my mother. It was a bastion of middle-class respectability, and that was more important than anything else at all. Her aunt had been a lifelong music teacher. We got an upright piano when I was about eight or nine, and beginner music books, and I excitedly started on the first pages.

'You need to wait until you start lessons. You will get the hand position wrong otherwise,' my mother said, coming round the corner into the lounge, looming in the doorway.

I can still almost see the page of music in front of me. A tune from colonialist oppressive times, 'Indian Song'. The excitement of making music fades. This, like anything else in life, must be done 'right', and only our mother defines what 'right' is. Or rather, what 'wrong' is. There is no acknowledgement of my feelings of happiness, my excitement, my initiative. I never put my whole heart into learning piano after that, did not feel any natural talent, and often felt awkward and laboured at lessons. This wasn't helped by being hopelessly shortsighted, something not picked up until I was ten, when a school eye check revealed I could not even read the first letter on an eye chart. My piano teacher had 'wondered'. But said nothing.

After a few years of lessons, one summer at the start of the year, I begged to be allowed to stop. I had to ask my mother, I knew. Dad would have no influence here. It didn't even occur to me to ask him; my mother was so firmly in control of so much of our lives.

I burst into tears.

Mother looked dispassionate, disdainful, annoyed.

'You need to keep doing lessons until Grade 5. Once you've got to that level, you'll be able to pick it up again later in life.'

Piano lessons were continued. I passed Grade 5, not very well. I stopped lessons.

I have never wanted to play piano ever again. And I have no memory of ever crying again in front of my mother. There was no point.

I made a point of not insisting my kids ever continued with something they truly wanted to stop doing. I asked that they finish off the current term, or the season if it was a team sport. No more. A kid needs space to know what they want, and when they want to stop. It is such a basic life skill to give your child.

I cannot ever imagine forcing them against their will, in tears, to continue an optional activity.

THE SAFETY DRAGON

'Validation plays a huge role in recovery from emotional (or any other kind of) neglect, because the wound neglect inflicts on us is invalidation — of our needs, our problems, our very personhood...'

– Dr Glenn Doyle: Instagram, @DrDoyleSays, March 2024

In the middle of my four months of EMDR, things looked great, with quick progress in resolving some major symptoms. Panic attacks and anxiety in public settings have gone, some isolating behaviours are receding. But after three months I begin to have doubts that I can barely bring myself to face. I don't feel at all 'fixed', yet. The first therapist I asked about EMDR said that in the public sector, six sessions is the maximum, but in private work, she found clients needed an average of about ten. I'm well past ten sessions now.

Something's not right. Why am I still getting suicidal thoughts? Shutting down?

But we plough on with the protocol. We start our fifteenth week with this memory of my mother and me.

We'd used the container exercise to safely hold the painful emotions over to the next week. The therapist suggests in earlier sessions to make myself a 'safe place' in my mind, as a tool to be able to bear what came up in the session and in between.

I objected.

'Nowhere is safe. I carry this stuff in my mind; it's always with me'.

The word 'safe' is weirdly unsettling. I don't know, at this point, how common this is for survivors of childhood trauma. There is no 'safe' in my life. It's odd to suddenly realise that. It is a foreign concept, something with no real meaning to me, something I can't grasp. It is unfamiliar, and the unfamiliar makes me suspicious. Like the therapist is doing some kind of Jedi mind trick to control me. Safe is — somehow — not safe.

So, we try the container exercise instead.

'Imagine a container, it could be a box, a chest, whatever you like. Do you have a picture of one? What does it look like? Good. Imagine how it will be locked up and secured. Imagine where it will be. Realise that you are the one in control of it, only you have access to it. Got that? Good. Now try opening the lid, and putting in today's memory, and all the things that are too hard. Your box is big enough, yes?'

I struggle with this exercise. I see a large wooden chest, strongly studded and padlocked. Getting ephemeral things like thoughts inside feels odd. I try to conjure up imaginary scrolls and scraps of paper. It's still a struggle.

We try the container exercise especially when a session isn't long enough to fully 'process' the memory we're dealing with. Most memories seem okay to deal with in one session — mainly because I'm still guessing at what my feelings are about them, rather than allowing myself to feel the distress they cause. But this last one, the one about my mother and me when I was a little girl, this one takes two sessions.

'Try opening your container. Take your time putting this memory in. Is it safely put inside?'

'I'm not sure'.

The therapist looks thoughtful for a moment.

'You could have something to help guard the chest? Perhaps a dragon?'

My eyes light up, I smile. A dragon — perfect. A somewhat cartoon version springs to mind, a dragon about the size of the chest, black, large-eyed, with an attitude but clearly knowing I'm his master — a kind of, 'I've got this, boss' feel. It helps.

In the next session the therapist offers the technique of 'strengths work', finding strength from supportive figures from my childhood, even if they weren't there in the scene from my memory. I reflect that supportive figures were distinctly lacking in my childhood. I recall staying a few days with my sister at Aunty Cate's place, with her husband and son, on our return from Jamaica. My parents weren't with us, I think because they were looking for a place to stay. I have a strong but vague memory of feeling warm and loved and safe, of sitting on someone's lap, of feeling cared about, in a way that seemed unusual. But after that my parents chose a place right across the other side of the sprawling metropolis of Auckland,

and I have no memory of ever being with Aunty Cate again without my mother also being there. Contact with any other relative was sporadic. I suspect those who could, kept visits to our place to a minimum. When visiting other older relatives, it was always with my mother. I don't remember anyone coming to babysit me, ever. Technically my next-oldest sister was old enough to babysit, at least when she wasn't confined to a psychiatric ward, but I don't remember that happening.

We open my dragon-guarded imaginary container and restart processing the memory.

When I was somewhere between seven and ten, I got measles. I'd been sick the day before. Mother came into my darkened bedroom the next morning, unusual for her, to check on me. I remember her face looming over me in the darkened room.

She laughed.

Without saying a word to me, my mother left my bedroom. I could hear her telling the rest of the family, laughing. 'Robyn's got measles!'

She did come back, telling me the curtains will stay pulled, that I can't read, that measles might hurt my eyes otherwise. She fetches me a lemonade ice block from the dairy just two doors away from us, to keep my liquids up. I'm surprised at the treat.

But what really hits me is the memory of that face looming over mine in the darkness, that feeling of utter, terrifying alone-ness, powerlessness, that barely recognised shame of being laughed at just for being sick. There were no kind words, no commiseration, no asking what I needed, no acknowledging that being sick and not being able to read would be hard for me, an avid reader. I was, technically, physically 'looked after': but I did not feel looked after. I felt utterly abandoned by the one who, above all others, was meant to be there for me.

The therapist suggests I imagine who else could stand there by my bed that day — my adult self? I slump on the couch in her office, feeling defeated, overwhelmed by the feeling I have pushed away for nearly fifty years. She pushes the box of tissues towards me. I feel angry at her question.

'Yes, me, and my four grown-up kids, and my two friends, my husband... It's not rocket science! How hard is it to show a bit of kindness and understanding to a sick child?'

'That's a lot of people you have, to show up for your younger self. That's great!' she enthuses.

'I think you were emotionally neglected every day of your childhood,' she goes on.

She looks thoughtful.

'We could go on doing EMDR forever, really. I guess at some point you need to decide how much you want to do, how much of the symptoms you can bear.'

We agree that a session next week, the last available before her month-long holiday, is not needed. But inside, I'm beginning to reel. EMDR hasn't worked. It hasn't fixed me completely. And now, once again, I face a long break without support. There is no plan in place to support me, other than the reminder to ring the community mental health team, should I 'need' it. No appointment made for her return.

At a similar age to me getting measles, my youngest daughter needed major, urgent, risky spinal surgery.

She fondly reminisces about the hot chocolate drinks we had together at the hospital cafe after appointments, the debriefing we did, the time I spent with her, supporting her. I reflect that I sometimes erred by telling her at times that 'it could be worse — at least they got it in time to keep you out of a wheelchair, at least you're not also got some other major condition like that child in the room next door with a missing limb'. She laughs and reminds me that she felt able to push back on those statements. She felt supported, even if I didn't get it perfectly right.

I cannot, ever, imagine having this kind of conversation with my mother, who couldn't even handle a simple case of measles, emotionally. I had to cope with something far harder, as many, many parents do. It's your job. You may not like it, you may not think you'll cope with the anguish of seeing your child on the operating table for a risky and rare operation, you don't know how to face being told by the pale, focused recovery nurse of her screams of pain on waking, you never imagined having to coach her through breathing exercises you learned to deal with labour pain, when she is just ten, and the nurse needs her on her back to be wheeled to the ward. And yet you do. It would seem monstrous not to.

In the same month as my EMDR therapy is coming to an end, I get a memoir from a complex trauma survivor out from the library.* I heard about it on YouTube. The author, Stephanie Foo, went through a very different childhood to mine. I do relate to her feeling that 'other people had it worse'. And then, her description of her EMDR leaps off the page, and I almost jump in the air in excitement, pointing. Look, there's why it wasn't working for me too! That inability to rate how distressing a memory is spot on. No-one else I know has done EMDR, I have no-one to compare notes with, but now finally, buried in the pages of this memoir, I feel seen.

This shows me the power of sharing stories. I tell a close supporter once more that I must write up my experiences and share them. She is affirming, repeating over the coming months, 'Are you still taking notes, Robyn? Your story needs to be told. It would be so helpful.'

---

* Stephanie Foo's ground-breaking *What My Bones Know: A Memoir of Healing From Complex Trauma*, published just a year earlier in 2022.

CHILDHOOD IN PARADISE

'My clinical experience with those who have suffered severe neglect is that recovery is harder in many ways than for those who suffered abuse because you can look and say <u>that</u> shouldn't have happened, but how do you look over there and say <u>that should have</u>, when you don't even know what it is.'

— Dr Diane Langberg: YouTube, 10 May 2017: 'Lessons from a Life of Counselling — Diane Langberg', @HelpingUpMission

I don't remember all that much from our family's stay in Jamaica.

I remember missing the taste of mangoes fresh from the tree, when we returned to New Zealand just as I turned six. I have a love of lush gardens full of plants and tropical vibes, something luckily obtainable even as far south as Wellington, in my country.

At age four and a half, I attended the Peter Pan Preparatory School, following the English schooling system. I remember the shock of being separated from a classmate, for talking too much. Age five.

I remember his name, look him up online. He's become the (former Director-General of Health) Ashley Bloomfield of his place of residence overseas: he speaks on a radio or podcast programme about the nature of life with COVID now becoming endemic rather than pandemic in nature.

For years afterwards, my school reports mention that I am a 'quiet' student.

I remember going to see *Jesus Christ Superstar* at a drive-in. Just one scene is all I recall, a panned-out shot of Jesus being flogged, and the signature tune for the show blaring over the top. But the year after my election loss, I wonder. This clearly scared me, a lot. And not surprising — Mel Gibson's *The Passion* was hard to stomach even for many adults. The story is gruesome. But what would it feel like to watch that scene now, as a grown-up? I get out my phone with its five-and-a-half-inch screen, find a video clip of the scene I want.

The first sensation is puzzled amazement. This 70s movie looks horribly cheap by today's standards, and rather more camp than frightening. The 'Superstar' song doesn't even play during the flogging scene. What's up?

And then — a single second of the scene catches my breath, and there I am again, a scared, small five-year-old, watching this not in the safety of my own lounge as an adult, but trapped in the family car, looking at the most enormous screen I would ever have seen in my short life, in colour. We didn't get a colour TV until we returned to New Zealand: I remember the shock of seeing Big Bird in colour on a TV in England when we went for a trip, when I was about four or five. Kids weren't accustomed to a life of screens, certainly not the size of a drive-in. A TV over about 25 inches was unheard of.

I don't remember anyone turning round to check on me in the back seat, or afterwards. I was only five. I wouldn't take my kids to a big-screen version of the life of Jesus at that age. It's too much. And this is a great lesson for me right now: what my child-self saw and felt is so much more than what my adult self would experience. It's easy to forget how little I once was, how powerless, how few options I had, how overwhelmingly big and scary things could be that wouldn't be to grown-up me. I'm learning to take the little-me version of events far more seriously. I learn that if I'm recalling a memory, it is telling me something vitally important, because there doesn't seem to be many memories at all. These memories are precious clues, fragmented, hard to place in time, but very real.

I remember coming home from school in Jamaica one day to discover a whole crowd of people on our wide tiled veranda: my mother had been held at knifepoint at the washing line, a maid had chased the would-be robber in her sports car, the thief had dropped most of the contents of the stolen handbag in the chase. This wasn't our first robbery — there'd been two others in our three-year stay. Jamaica was newly independent but suffering the effects of the slave trade, of colonisation. It was 'normal' for us as a white family to have local black Jamaicans as servants, even if paid. Mother clearly saw herself as superior to them. She liked giving orders, feeling like someone of higher status.

I don't recall being frightened at all for my mother's safety. She seemed to be relishing the attention, repeating the story, oblivious to anyone else. There was a sense of surprise, shock. Nothing more.

I don't remember but was told about my sister June carrying me in the street in Jamaica, and a passer-by saying, 'What a lovely son you have!'

I always had short hair as a child, we all did. According to my sister, our mother saw long hair was something hippies had, and our family were above that. Sex, drugs, and rock 'n roll, were all for people from an inferior class. June told me that she had bought her first pair of jeans with her own money but discovered them missing on arrival in Jamaica. Our mother had deliberately left them behind or thrown them out. Jeans were 'working class', and her daughters weren't. That changed by the time I was a teenager — at least, the jeans part. I was allowed to wear jeans. But it doesn't surprise me that I've worn them almost every day of my adult life.

I do remember the time I felt volcanic anger at our mother.

June had been in an argument with our mother, June then sixteen or seventeen, me four or five. June, myself, and my other sister had retreated to a bedroom. I remember hiding behind a glory box, saying loudly, 'We should call the police!' I was wildly angry.

And then Mother stormed into the room, headed straight for June around the end of the bed, furthest away from my hiding place. She raises her hand to strike. I can feel the terror; I'm exiting my body, my memory sees me from a short distance above, a small, angry but now terrified child cowering behind a chest, seeing her beloved older sister about to be hit. My memory abruptly cuts off there. I don't remember the blow.

I asked June recently about this.

'Did Mum hit you? I don't remember that part.'

'Oh yes,' she said, her face blank. 'I expected to be hit at home if we misbehaved; we were caned in school back then for discipline.'

My heart sinks. Just because it was legal and socially acceptable to physically discipline your children back in the 70s doesn't make it right. And June wasn't a child. She was a teenager, on the brink of leaving home entirely, practically an adult. Had our mother hit any other seventeen-year-old, it would have been criminal assault.

'It felt terrifying to me. I was only little!' I replied.

My sister clearly hasn't ever thought about it like that. But she said that was why she left home: our mother had only one way of doing things, only her way was 'right', and June had discovered by being among friends in Jamaica that their families did do things differently. She had, unexpectedly, been given a lot of freedom, and was very social. She wanted some things to be different; she just couldn't handle the arguments with our mother to try to change anything. When her boyfriend left Jamaica for another country and then wrote asking her to follow him, she left, with our parents' consent, aged just seventeen.

I ask Tina about our mother's hitting June.

'Oh yes, she hit me too. Someone had accused me of stealing something that had gone missing and had told Mum. She hit me on the arm. I was about seventeen'.

I have no memory of June leaving us. I was five years old.

The next time I saw June, I was eleven.

Until then we had only brief, awkward moments on the old-style telephone, cord attached to the hallway wall. Everyone in the family stood round as we'd been told to by our excited mother, waiting to talk to June on the expensive long-distance toll call. June's voice sounded such a long way away, in an unfamiliar Canadian accent, talking mostly about their snowfalls. Her life was strange to me in our semi-tropical city. She was a stranger to me. From my early teens she started regular duty visits back home, every few years, bringing her first child, her second child, her second husband. I don't recall getting to know her really until she came to help with the birth of my third child, many years later.

I didn't fully grasp just how much I'd lost in my childhood. I couldn't face that reality. The one person my infant self probably saw as a caring mother figure had gone from my life all too early; and life was only going to get scarier at home.

DARKEST AFTER DAWN

'It's not only trauma people are healing from, but the ways people treated them when they asked for help.'

— Nate Postlethwait: Instagram,
5 August 2024, @nate_postlethwt

A couple of nights' broken sleep, a day of feeling suicidal once more, leave me terrified of getting worse. I return to the GP for sleeping tablets, just in case, just a very small number so there can be no overdose risk. This time it's a different doctor, and all seems fine until I get home. I go over the conversation in my mind. I have a lightbulb moment. I think, from overthinking one of our interactions, that the doctors know something they're not telling me... I am more at risk than I think, and they know it... I pull out my tablet and start searching the net.

Shit.

There it is, clear and scientifically described, in detail: a scholarly article about a hospital's inability to prevent the death by suicide of someone, in a way I realise I could very easily replicate. I could overdose on a prescription drug regularly given to a household member, not the one-off sleeping tablets but another drug. My mind reels. Surely the GPs would be aware of this risk? Why haven't they said anything? For reasons that seem rational in my state of mind, I feel this method is an acceptable way to go. And it seems highly likely to work. It ticks all my boxes.

This, this is how I'd do it. This is it.

And the GPs I've seen so far either don't know or don't want to tell me about this risk.

Right now, it's inescapably an option, detailed, and clear, and highly achievable: the only question is now: do I want to use it?

I sit with this knowledge, leaning forward in my swivel armchair in our lounge, knowing I have what I need to kill myself, right here, and the doctors hadn't even bothered to check on the risk this poses to me.

Life feels like it couldn't get any more unreal.

I sit in shock.

Do I do the right thing? Do I turn myself in, own up to what I have, what I now know?

Do I keep this stuff for a rainy day? The lure of having a kind of insurance policy — if everything gets too tough, I have a way out —

is strong, even on that sunny morning in my lounge, when I feel reasonably okay compared to many days.

I'm about to go visit a close friend. It would feel somehow like betrayal to turn up and pretend nothing has happened.

With a little difficulty, I choose honesty.

I drive to my friend's house, ask for her opinion. Am I right to be mad at the doctors for putting me in this position, for being so tied up with my depressive symptoms and with their assessment of me as low risk, without doing anything to reduce that risk? I hand over my ticket to freedom from pain, the means I've just identified, spurred on by adrenaline and support.

I regret that decision numerous times in the weeks to come. It's hard to lose control. It's hard to lose the calmness that comes with seeing an end in sight, even if I'm not a hundred per cent sure I'd do it. I'm resentful that the option is no longer at hand.

A couple of days later, another (un)helpful a-ha! moment.

I can start again! I still have ongoing access to the means of choice.

No-one has thought to question this, not friends or family whom I've told.

And so, the decision must be made over again, every day.

I'm weirdly both upset that no one else has thought of this catch, despite how open I've been about it all, and relieved.

Look, I think — I'm still smarter than them all. I can still figure this out better than anyone.

It's a twisted logic that still makes perfect sense to me. This is my life — my childhood — on replay: being the one who must call for help, being the one who sees the grown-ups around her incapable or distracted by others with greater needs, being the one who knows no help is really coming.

Within a week or two, I start again on gathering my means of choice. Now, the countdown is on.

I cancel a planned trip overseas, one postponed from the previous year due to the Omicron COVID variant outbreak. There's no way I could fly, alone, for hours. I'm exhausted, often with tense muscles, broken sleep, shutting down. I'm gutted. This is an experience I'll never get the chance to have again.

My EMDR provider is away for a whole month. We'd reached sixteen sessions by this point, four months of therapy.

Around weeks four and five, I experience major breakthroughs — I suddenly stop having panic attacks going out in public, I can look people in the eye again, I restart some social contact that has been missing for five months. It seems like a miracle: but it's not enough. The suicidal thoughts return. There doesn't seem to be any plan, except perhaps more EMDR.

The disappointment is too hard to take in. I now must face facts. EMDR isn't the magic solution I so hoped it would be. This health worker has also touched on another mode of therapy with me, dialectical behavioural therapy, but there's no suggestion that she expects me back as a client, no real plan going forward while she's away, and once more, the bottom falls out of my world.

I know I need more help. The between-sessions support phone number she gives me is for the local community mental health team, the crisis team. This team the helplines constantly refer to in their automated messages.

Two days later I think I'm in enough of a crisis to call the community team. Where else is left, when I don't trust the GPs I've seen, when my therapy provider is away, when I know that helplines are of so little use to me that they feel like I'm playing Russian roulette?

So finally, I ring. I can barely speak. I'm home alone, sitting on the swivel chair in the lounge.

There's no option to text. It takes forty minutes of conversation before I'm convinced that it's safe to offer my name, that there's any hope using this service.

We discuss what I need — no medication, just regular support until I find more therapy.

I'm told, explicitly, that this is possible. There's an apology, he'd like me to be seen next week but there's a delay due to high demand, so it may be 'a few weeks'. I end the call by pointing out that if it's more than four weeks away, that is dangerous for me.

The next week the appointment letter comes. My appointment — for an initial assessment by the service, in person — is seven weeks away from when I called them for help.

Seven. Weeks.

And this isn't too bad — a news report around this time says that the current wait for this service for someone under eighteen is now ten weeks.*

One week later, I'm back determinedly gathering means to die. I know this is not good.

I call the local crisis line again, as the letter said to do if I needed to while waiting to be seen.

A different man on the end of the phone, and he sounds about as depressed as me.

'We're overloaded,' he says despondently. He perks up. 'How about ringing 1737?'

I point out that I tried this, months ago, and it didn't help.

All he can offer is to email the team to bump me up the waiting list, if someone else pulls out. He doesn't sound at all hopeful this will do any good.

I think now, when it comes to asking for help, I've finally reached rock bottom. I'm actively suicidal, an attempt feels like only a matter of a few weeks away, and the only appointment I have

---

* *New Zealand Herald*, 15 June 2023:
https://www.nzherald.co.nz/nz/politics/youth-mental-health-wait-times-in-wellington-more-than-double/MRO66TVICJF55CXONJVIIBMNGA/

is for some weeks after that. WTF? How is someone in distress supposed to survive this?

I feel like a robot. At times I can no longer sense the sunlight on me, I see no point in attempts at socialising, or doing anything, my muscles are tense, my whole being exhausted. I often imagine horrible things happening to me, like being put in a psychiatric ward, as my sister was. It is obvious to those around me that I'm not doing well. The length of wait to get help is weighing on everyone. My family makes an extra effort to show me that they love me, that they notice I'm not okay, that they're there for me and mad with me at the system.

But I haven't told anyone what I'm doing in secret, preparing to die.

A calm descends at times. I get seen for other health needs — a cataract is noticed at a routine check-up, I send a grumpy email to the menopause clinic about some poor information, I make an appointment to a different hormone clinic. Details about a proposed complaint meeting at the doctors are arranged.

A video call from a far-flung family member, the first from her in months, outs the truth.

She asks point blank: do you have a plan? — yes. Shock and surprise registers.

Do you know how you'll do it? — yes.

I can see on my phone, my idiotically smiling face in the small window on top of the larger one showing my relative's very concerned face. I'm smiling, oddly, at how clever I've been — look, you're the first person to ask — I'm smiling, awkwardly, because it is the most awkward conversation ever, for many reasons: I'm smiling perhaps, maybe, in a little relief. Because now someone knows.

I promise to dispose of what I've got. I do so.

Some days later, I start again. I can't handle not having the option open to me.

I can't handle this numbness, this thin covering over a chasm of pain.

In a more lucid moment amid the emotional chaos, I ring the Health and Disability Commissioner, a body that helps with making complaints about health services. In the mud and darkness waiting for an ambulance at the bottom of the cliff, this service shines. The response of the woman on the phone is very practical, and further help is offered if needed. I'm told to be specific — dates, times, names — and to state specifically what I want as outcomes from the process. I rewrite my letter and make a formal complaint to my medical centre. It turns out to be life-savingly effective.

The day arrives for my complaint meeting. I take one of my adult daughters as a support person, and she's dressed in corporate workwear, looking like a lawyer. We're taken to a back room, given some written responses to go over, and then we wait until the person hearing our complaint is free.

The room is very small. I feel confident, some angry energy going through me.

The meeting starts awkwardly.

'So, how do you two know each other?' I'm asked.

'She's here to support me,' I glare, sidestepping an answer.

My trust most definitely must be earned, at this point.

The tone changes quickly.

'I want you to know how very, very grateful we are that we can learn from this situation ... with no harm done... no permanent harm.' Eyes look deep into mine. 'Very grateful.'

It's described to me that there have already been steps taken to review my case, to learn from it. I discuss how concerned I was about the depression being the focus, about how I didn't feel the risk assessment for suicide was a good focus, that there was not enough risk reduction. I'm met with great understanding — 'Yes, trauma makes you more volatile, any appointment is only a snapshot in time…no, sadly, doctors don't get teaching about [psychological] trauma in their training…'

We discuss who will be my doctor in future. My daughter and I leave, satisfied. The complaint was taken seriously. I feel seen, understood.

I'm not asked directly, and I don't volunteer about my currently active suicidality, but it abruptly stops that day. The simplest of interventions in some ways, the most complex to provide, in others: a human being who cares, understands, and makes me feel seen as an individual, as someone carrying the load of past trauma.

Which is just as well, because worse is ahead.

My daughter and I sit on our sunny window seat, comparing notes. The person who saw us for the complaint was amazing, we both agree. I off-handedly comment that they didn't address the issue of what to do if I were to keep on gathering the means available — in other words, if I were actively suicidal. She looks at me in mild surprise:

'But Mum, if you were doing that, you'd already be in a psych ward!'

My level of self-disclosure is rocketing lately.

'I'd already been doing that for weeks,' I say drily. She looks a bit stunned and does not reply.

Another family member enters the room, and the conversation moves away to other topics.

IN LIVING MEMORY

'Childhood trauma isn't something you just get over as you grow up...
The single most important thing that we need today is to look this problem in the face and say this is real, this is all of us.'

— Dr Nadine Burke Harris: YouTube, 'How childhood trauma affects health across a lifetime', 18 February 2015, @TED

It's hard to get funding for mental health treatment in our country, like many. New Zealand has a special quirk called ACC — the Accident Compensation Corporation.* More than once, a health professional warned me off even trying this route to get financial support for treatment, as being too traumatic. And in my assessment, the emotional neglect, the trauma of seeing family violence, all predates any memory of sexual abuse, which means no ACC cover. Until I was in my mid-thirties I did not even recognise or remember any sexual abuse in my childhood. The realisation that I was wrong about this rocked my world to its core.

In 2005, a prominent New Zealander lost name suppression and pleaded guilty to charges of indecently assaulting young girls.†

The country was horrified, indignant. This man had been leader of a religious-based political party, a moral crusader, a husband and father of ten. One day I idly glanced over the details of his offending. I think this must be the first time I have ever read these kinds of details in print. First in the list of his crimes were instances of him reaching into a young girl's underwear and touching her genitals.

What's so criminal about that? I thought.

Something about my reaction felt very, very wrong.

Wait — that's a — crime?

And suddenly, about thirty years after the event, a lost memory hit me hard.

I rang my sister Tina.

'I found this photo of Ozzy in Mum's things,' I said, keeping it light and casual. 'Do you remember him?'

---

* Accident Compensation Corporation, set up in 1974 after decades of no-fault worker injury compensation. The right to take a claim through the courts for physical or mental injury was removed. The ability to claim compensation for mental injury was gradually added in limited circumstances, called 'sensitive claims'. For childhood trauma, you must prove a mental injury clearly resulted from sexual abuse or a physical injury, and the pathway to proving this is recognised as retraumatising.
† See Wikipedia entry for Graham Capill: https://en.wikipedia.org/wiki/Graham_Capill

'Oh yes. He used to love having you sit in his lap,' she replied. I moved the conversation on. I had the proof I needed about what I now remembered.

Ozzy and his wife, a retired couple, used to visit us when I was in primary school, friends of our family.

I have only one memory of him.

I was lying across our four-seater couch in our lounge. My head was in his lap. And then, for a moment, his hand went down my pants, touching me.

In my memory, I get up at once and leave, knowing instinctively, horrifyingly, that this is not right. But the memory cuts out there. I know I told no-one; I think no-one else was in the lounge at the time. I can't recall whether I stopped sitting near him or on his lap from then on. I have no memory of anyone noticing any change in my behaviour to him. But what I now realise is that I was so emotionally deprived that I went looking for love from somewhere else, and that his touching me wasn't just horrible. It was a crime.

By the time this memory comes back to me I have four young children of my own. I watch my offspring like a hawk, anxious for any sign of possible abuse, hovering near any adult male whatsoever who comes to our house. It takes years to relax, years to realise that my children are nowhere near as much at risk as I was, for the simple reason that they feel loved by their parents. My husband tells them so verbally every day, he hugs them every day, I do the same. They have no reason to look for other adults to fill the void.

One day after this my child brings home from school a worksheet about keeping safe. It explains in simple but effective terms that no-one, no-one, should touch their body, especially the private parts that we keep covered, unless for medical reasons, and never as a secret. That if anyone does so — babysitter, uncle, whoever — they are to find a trusted adult to tell, and if they're not believed, to find someone else to tell, until they get help.

There was nothing like this in my childhood. I am deeply

grateful my children have this added protection also. I check in — 'Have you been touched like that, ever? No? Great!'

I wonder who I might have told. It would never have occurred to me to talk to a grown-up. Certainly not my mother. My father? In my eyes, this was a friend of my parents. Would I have told my father what their friend did to me?

I'm left reeling from the recovery of this memory, repressed so long.

I seek help from a fellow church member, someone who I think will understand. I'm grateful for feeling safe enough to talk. But during this, the church member suggests that I picture myself back then, and picture that Jesus was in the room too.

I recoiled in horror at this thought.

'What, like a pervert? Jesus didn't stop this guy. No-one noticed. God wasn't there!'

I'm angry, I don't have the words for it back then, but I feel like this is gaslighting or spiritual bypassing. Pretending it was okay because Jesus was there and didn't approve. It feels horribly off. How could someone who is supposed to love me stand back and do nothing?

Years later, in that first therapy session after my election loss, the therapist — also a Christian — tries a similar tack. It still feels totally off. This is not right, and it is not therapy. It is a sick, misguided, fumbling attempt to answer, in the face of deepest pain, why God allows suffering. I do not go back again.

I read recently and with horror about how the recovery of repressed memories have been weaponised against victims down the ages, from Freud to twentieth-century America.[*] There is good evidence that recovered memories are not made up. There may be chronological issues, as trauma memories do not form a neat narrative, have gaps, and often a muddled timeframe. That makes

---

[*] Anna Holtzman, 14 February 2020: https://medium.com/fourth-wave/harvey-weinsteins-false-memory-defense-and-its-shocking-origin-story-2b0e4b98d526

sense. The mind is trying to block out something horrific, something overwhelming, unspeakably awful. But the body remembers, the brain eventually may recall some of the awful truth, and when it does, your world can never be the same.

IT'S ON YOUR GENES

'We have drunk from the cup of affliction...'

— Giuseppe Verdi: *Speed Your Journey*, from 'Nabucco'

Just a couple of weeks after the election loss, a distant relative got in touch.

'Hi Robyn, I've been reading a book called "It Didn't Start with You" by Mark Wolynn. It's about epigenetics... I've been quite impacted by it on a personal level and have developed a keen interest in the family history. I remembered you have a wealth of knowledge re the family tree and have sent me a few things over the years. I'd be very keen to have a chat with you at some stage, to hear more detail about what you have discovered!'

I sit back, phone in hand, amazed.

Genealogy has often been the obsession that gives me a family I never had. It's also the thrill of playing detective, of finding out things no-one has ever known, of fact-checking, uncovering the truth. Stories and patterns and origins. Reminders that I am part of a family, we once lived in villages, we once knew each other well and saw each other daily. History and change, reasons for travelling halfway across the globe in wooden sailing ships and steamships. Many of the living seem unconcerned about the dead, but to me they're more dear and closer than most relatives I've encountered in childhood.

Share some family history... share the stories of heartache and loss and success...

Sure, how long have you got?

There's a grave just half an hour's drive from my house that I've taken my kids to more than once. *Sleep on, Beloved* reads the epitaph, aching with loss. The year is 1927, the year that deaths of women post childbirth from sepsis or septicaemia came to a peak in our country — seventy women. Less than a hundred years ago, health professionals still refused to accept the basics of handwashing in health. My grandmother had birthed her fourth son, in hospital as was the new-fangled convention. Hands were unlikely to be washed. Two weeks later she was dead.

Sepsis is a hideous way to die.

My father was seven years old.

Dad along with his elder brother was sent to boarding school in the South Island, a long journey away from his Wellington family home. There later was a stepmother, with two children from a previous marriage. Dad did not speak of his childhood to me, other than a story about not being told by his father why he couldn't have the bicycle he wanted (too expensive, apparently). There were no other relatives out here in the Antipodes: my dad's parents emigrated right at the start of the First World War. Dad was born at the end of the war, in England. The shocking loss of his mother reverberates down the years. My mother expressed anger that a letter my father wrote as an anguished little boy to his dying mother in hospital is in the hands of other family members. Dad was always quiet, reserved, and somewhat awkward in social situations at times. He served in the army in the Second World War but didn't see any military action.

His father, my grandfather, served in the field ambulance corps for New Zealand in the First World War. One of his uncles also served, with the British Army. Both these brothers, according to their military records, would have seen the horrors of the Western Front. Both were unable to return to England for their father's funeral in 1917. This man, my great-grandfather, was the first in his family to get an education, to leave the close-knit village our family had been in for hundreds of years.

Three generations is not enough time to adapt to living without family support.

There is my great-great-grandfather, who died in his late twenties of wounds at sea. He was merely an able seaman, the lowest rank. But on his only child's marriage certificate his occupation is named as 'Master Mariner' — a sea captain. Maybe his widow chose to upgrade his rank to provide some solace to herself and her daughter.

No wonder the echoes of trauma are there.

. . .

As for my mother's side... there is plenty of trauma here, too.

I remember Mother proudly showing me family tree records she had gathered, everything neatly labelled and sorted into folders, preprinted genealogical charts and forms filled out, precise, orderly, and utterly wrong.

She pointed out the branch that supposedly came from landed gentry in England. Their elder brother was the squire of Evesham, his family line going back in gentrified manner, with a governor of the Bank of England here, or a Simon de Montfort supporter there. The younger brothers, so the family record went, came to Tasmania.

The truth was quite different. The elder brother was shipped to Tasmania from England at age seventeen, a convict, having stolen five shawls: his term of punishment was seven years. He had lived in the poverty-stricken East End of London, not the vale of Evesham. He was a cripple, proved unsatisfactory as help on colonists' farms, and got sent to the notoriously evil prison at Port Arthur. He died young, having run pubs after his release. His younger brothers did come out to join him. The shame was so heavy that a story was made up, and the following generations believed it: wilfully, naively, shamefully ignorant of their convict heritage.

> *The idea that convicts might have a history worth telling was foreign in the Australia of the 1950s and 1960s.... [O]n the feelings and experiences of these men and women, little was written. They were statistics, absences, and finally embarrassments.... The idea of the 'convict stain,' a moral blot soaked into our fabric, dominated all argument about Australian selfhood....**

My mother spent hundreds and hundreds of dollars while I was growing up in Auckland, buying expensive, garishly decorated Royal Worcester plates with an 'Evesham' pattern. She idolised this

---

* Robert Hughes, *The Fatal Shore* (Collins Harvill, London, 1986).

reminder of her genteel heritage. No-one could make a loud noise of plate on plate without her furious, hurt tone, a reprimand to be careful. Each dinner plate was stored with their original plastic bag in between them.

Without asking me, she determined that I would inherit the collection. Dutifully I brought it down to Wellington when she went into care in the rest home. Dinner plates, lunch plates, side plates, dessert bowls, soup bowls, sauce jugs, gravy jugs, servers, casserole dishes. I deliberately put them through the dishwasher, which faded the garish pattern, but did not break the plates as I had hoped.

It took me till fifteen years after her death to realise I could just get rid of them. I gleefully gave almost all of them away and bought cheap plain white replacements. They soon chipped. I didn't care.

Thankfully my mother died before the height of my family tree research, before DNA tests put me in touch with an Australian cousin who was not ashamed to face the truth. And before I found that another line of my mother's also came as convicts, this time from Scotland, having stolen a watch.

These were both on my mother's mother's side: but there was tragedy and poverty on the father's side, too. My great-great-grandfather, a Cornish carpenter, died of a fever on the sailing ship that also brought his wife and one-year-old son to New Zealand, the other side of the world. The ship had suffered during heavy storms; it was not the only death. I cannot imagine how hard that would be, my great-great-grandmother and her infant son, alone in a strange land. She became a cook on a sheep station, I think, to keep her son with her.

Yes, I think I have a few trauma stories for you.

WAITING, AGAIN

'Complex trauma is chronic, repetitive, and relational in nature. It is one thing for example to experience significant trauma when you've been bombed or shot at by a faceless enemy but it is a completely different thing to be a developing child and the bomb and the gun in the form of physical abuse, sexual abuse, or severe neglect, come from your caregiver and never stop.'

— Dr Diane Langberg: YouTube, 'What forms of trauma go beyond PTSD?', 22 January 2016, @FOCLOnline

The Community Mental Health Team gives their prospective clients plenty of reading material for the long wait to see them. The letterhead for the appointment states the name as the 'Mental Health, Addictions and Intellectual Disability Service' — no Oxford comma for this department. It feels like an odd grab-bag.

The envelope spills out an intimidating pile of five booklets, in addition to the letter with the brief but disturbing details of my appointment in the far future. I wonder what people with limited literacy make of all this. It's hard enough for me to digest, in my state, and I have three university qualifications.

One booklet outlines information about the Team. One is from the Privacy Commissioner — *YOUR HEALTH INFORMATION: Know Your Privacy Rights*, as if all caps will induce me to read it now, when I care — at best — about survival rather than the privilege of privacy. One from a support charity that originally started as Schizophrenia Fellowship, Wellington Branch, though this part is hard to read as there is small black text on a dark teal background: one from the Health and Disability Commissioner — *Code of Health and Disability Services: Consumers' Rights* — apparently, I am a 'consumer' and have ten rights, at least.

Later, the Right number 4 paragraph (4) catches my eye.

'Every consumer has the right to have services provided in a manner that minimises the potential harm to, and optimises the quality of life of, that consumer.'

We're not off to a great start, as waiting seven weeks for a crisis service while being actively suicidal for several of those doesn't seem to meet the criteria of minimising harm, somehow. And the 'consumer' terminology feels... very 1990s managerial speak. Just a couple of decades past its use-by. So far, I don't feel I've 'consumed' anything but the very last dregs of my energy and patience.

There are also four pages of forms. I am supposed to fill these out and bring them to my appointment. The first is titled, 'LIFESTYLE SELF INVENTORY' in a quirky all-caps font that belongs more on a circus poster. It has fifteen questions helpfully labelled by subject — 'Desire to work: How much do I want to work?' being the top of the list. There is a scale from 0 to 10, individually labelled for each question.

I am supposed to rate these areas while 'thinking about your current situation'. I am at a loss. Do they want me to wait the remaining six weeks until just before the appointment, then fill it in? Fill it in now? My self-assessment would change from week to week, day to day. I can't think in longer timeframes. My brain hurts too much.

I scan the form.

'Housing: (My living situation is secure and settled. E.g. renting, own house).' 1 to 10.

Although I'm out of work, my husband is a professional, and we inherited money years ago. Being the joint owner of our family home, with investments, I'd have to put a 10 on that.

And immediately I realise this would put me above the threshold for scoring as Severe, the highest category, especially as th next question is about Self Confidence, and that too, I would need to rate highly, if I'm being honest with them. Because, weirdly, I have discovered it is entirely possible to fall apart mentally and still be self-confident.

I know, I have always known, it's not me who is at fault, even as a child. My first two therapists, with whom I only ever had one session, both denied this possibility, saying the 'younger me' would have felt this way even if adult me does not.[*] I have a deep suspicion, a core belief, *not* that *I* am unworthy or unlovable —

---

[*] American psychologist Dr Rick Hanson shares this unusual choice was his experience too: that while many kids make a fateful, unconscious choice that it must be them who is bad or crazy, not their parents, he did not. 'I don't know what enabled me at age six to have a crystal clear highly memorable experience in which I just became super clear that the sources of unhappiness in my family were not inside me...'. — 'Authentically Developing Self-Worth': Being Well Podcast, YouTube, 8 November 2022, @Forrest Hanson

unable to be loved — but that *the world* is not able to love me. I have little sense of self; I realise that later in therapy. But what little self there is does feel confident. I love public speaking, I was a community leader, I stood for political election. I don't suffer from much negative self-talk. I have a lot of criticism aimed at the outside world. Where does that figure in this quiz?

The last question is 'Mental Health (My mental health is stable.)'.

I am expected to rate this from 0 — not at all, to 10, very stable. Of all the questions this seems the most ridiculously irrelevant. Does anyone score themselves above a 3 — 'Slightly' stable — and still come to this service?

The bottom of this form gives the name of the New Zealand health professional who apparently wrote it in 2011, adapted from a 1992 form. A lot has happened in the field of mental health in the last twelve years, surely it is overdue for a revamp. Even just a change of font for the header?

The other form is simply titled 'DASS', which is not enlightening. The *very* fine print at the bottom of the page discloses that this is the Depression Anxiety Stress Scales questionnaire, from 1995. Among the questions from this thirty-year-old dinosaur are repeated questions about my view of my future but also, bizarrely, two on whether I have difficulty swallowing or have dryness of mouth. There are forty-two questions requiring a rating from 0 to 3. I don't even recognise that I'd recently done this same quiz, online.

'Do not spend too much time on any statement.'

I follow this instruction by not filling in the forms at all.

It feels like some kind of covert test — if you're mentally competent enough to fill out a form, maybe you show yourself as not in need of their services? I don't care. It's too much. I resign myself to the remaining weeks of waiting.

IN NEED OF A LITTLE DIVINATION

My long awaited first appointment with the community mental health team is a Friday morning. It's not at the local hospital, but a building in the nearby town centre. I take the lift, carefully waiting to go alone, so no-one can see where my destination is: arrive at the right floor, and nervously approach the reception desk.

This isn't like any regular health appointment. Walk in the main doors of any medical centre to see a GP, or into a hospital, and you could be there for anything, no judgement. We all need GPs and hospitals sometimes. But coming here, I feel like I'm forced to wear an emblazoned high-vis vest proclaiming that I am very mentally unwell, hopelessly addicted, or intellectually disabled. It feels unsettling. I don't want to be noticed in any of those ways.

I take a seat in a niche around a corner from the receptionist. I look up, and high on the opposite wall there's one of those concave mirrors usually seen at the bottom of awkward driveways or on especially bad road corners. There is no hiding in this place.

To start with I'm the only one there, and I sneak furtive looks at the grey carpet tiles, white institutional walls, the poster by the lift doors.

'Part of our job is to respond to urgent situations,' it announces, over a stylised picture of a large old-fashioned alarm clock.

'This may cause changes to scheduled appointments...'

Wait, whaaaatttt?

Even after a seven-week wait to see a crisis mental health service, there's the possibility of a last-minute postponement.

That, too, is unsettling.

The nurse comes out, apologising for the wait. It takes me a moment to realise she's talking about the minuscule seven-minute wait for this appointment to get underway, not the seven-week wait I've had to get to it. We take seats in a small, windowless grey room. She is patient, understanding, and thorough. She is not at all pleased with the treatment I received on my second phone call to the team — 'That should never have happened; may I raise that with the team? Do you want to make a complaint?' She never once mentions those forms I was supposed to fill in.

She's read the notes. She makes no comment on the tennis ball I carried in but that I put in my coat pocket on sitting down. She listens, and makes it clear it's okay to ramble off on a tangent when answering her questions for which she invariably apologises for having to ask, and to which she makes it clear I don't need to answer if it's too hard, especially around the childhood trauma. I had stopped myself and said she'd want to get back to her question, and she said, no, this is 'your time'. That phrase just about undoes me. It's so much the opposite of form-filling, it is incredibly powerful, and any last reserve about sharing simply melts away.

She knows how to get specific around the question of being suicidal and how to be gentle. I explain at one point the locked box offsite storage solution I came up with for my stash, and she replied, 'Oh yes, we use that here.' I felt like I've come home — here I don't need to explain why that works or what it means.

At one point she catches my inference that I'm unsure I meet the criteria for needing the team's help. She firmly reassures that I most certainly do meet the criteria; in fact, I need help urgently and it's now her job to make sure I get it. She explains the intricacies of this — how the Emergency Department at the main hospital is an option, really just a last resort and not ideal, but does keep you safe: how it might be the crisis team that sees me, but it might be an urgent appointment with a team psychiatrist, and I may be swapped from one to the other but it will be okay...

She asks what I want from them. I say I want monitoring, regularly, not from random individuals I must call up and repeat my story to; I want support figuring out what next; I want help applying for ACC funding.* I don't want my family to be placed in the position of having to ask the specifics of suicide to me, and she understands. 'They're there for emotional support.'

She concludes by affirming that I do need help from the team, and the only reason to delay seeing them until Monday is that I'm currently suicidal but not actively so, and I have family support for the weekend. She tells me to expect a phone call from the crisis team then. She agrees to my request that the person from the crisis team contacting me will text first, as I am finding phone calls coming at an unknown time to be stressful, even triggering.

There's a small warmth inside, a small hope, kindled by this calm, competent, understanding nurse. But I can't take in the explanation given of how their service is structured. It seems like this office I've come to today is some kind of second-tier gateway to a quite separate service, the crisis team, who do the initial care and then would pass me back to this community team, to someone like this nurse I've just met and bared all to for the last ninety minutes?

It feels like I'm in an old-fashioned arcade game, a ball being

---

* The Accident Compensation Corporation (ACC), as described earlier, is the New Zealand state entity responsible for administering the country's no-fault accidental injury compensation scheme, begun in 1974, that provides financial compensation and support to citizens, residents, and temporary visitors who have suffered personal injuries.

bounced around off a couple of different paddles and bumping into blockages, until I hit the right point of entry. Or is that exit? I'm confused, but I hear that help is — finally — coming.

I head home after going for a muffin and hot chocolate treat; I'm daring to feel slightly hopeful that I'm finally getting somewhere.

In the evening at home with family gathered, our youngest is our Dungeon Master in a second or third Dungeons & Dragons session we're squeezing in during a university break. As our adventure progresses, our whole party of iconic misfits fall down a trapdoor into magic-ridden dungeon rooms. All the magical traps get activated: we desperately need to know where the master key is to turn them off. My character, whom I've named Allvar Wisewater, an older male cleric, looks to the heavens, casts Divination and asks all the gods above where the key is and how to use it. Eloquent rhyming words come out of my surprised mouth to form the spell, which is not strictly necessary for game play but always fun for playing the part, when you can manage it.

My family around the table erupts in joy and applause. The Dungeon Master responds:

'Bookcase. Stone. .....'

The information saves the day and our party escapes in suitably dramatic last-minute fashion.

But weirdly, I blank out. A second after uttering my impromptu rhyming incantation, I can't recall a word of what I just said. Not even when I ask my daughter to repeat it for me.

I've dissociated, and part of the joy of the evening is robbed for me.

What did I just say? Why can't I remember it?

I text a friend. She initially misreads my mention of D&D as B&D, and we both have a laugh.

. . .

On Monday, I wait for the expected phone call from the crisis team, nerves on edge.

The call comes late in the morning.

There is no warning text, as we'd agreed there should be.

My senses are all on high alert, sensing danger, sensing incompetence, and they aren't disappointed.

The crisis team caller is a stranger, someone who has not met me or spoken to me before. She quickly asks a round of 'how likely are you to make an attempt' type questions, then says in an efficient business-like tone that I could get help — from another organisation. It's a charity that deals with women who have been sexually abused. She 'reassures' me that they understand suicidality.

'I will give you their number, you can ring them this afternoon, okay?' There's no hint of the crisis team or the community team, or whoever they are, being involved.

I'm being shoved off to yet another place, one that doesn't feel like a match to my needs. My main problem I believe is complex trauma, not sexual abuse. The distress, fear, and anger all ratchet up several notches very quickly, and I stumble out a response. I refuse.

'I've waited seven weeks to see your service. I was told on Friday I urgently need your service and would get help with your service, and now you're telling me to just phone somewhere else?'

I choke on a growing sob in my throat.

The caller hastily backtracks. She sounds alarmed, agrees to an in-person meeting the next day, gives rapid-fire instructions as to where to find the appointment location which I can barely keep track of, and ends the call.

I reach out once more to YouTube. I find a UK webinar on suicide risk assessment.[*]

---

[*] Assessment of Suicide Risk in Mental Health Practice: YouTube, 2023, @OxfordHealth. Video now unavailable. See Hawton, Keith et al. "Assessment of suicide risk in mental health practice: shifting from prediction to therapeutic assessment, formulation, and risk management." The Lancet. Psychiatry vol. 9,11 (2022): 922-928. doi:10.1016/S2215-0366(22)00232-2

Studies show that prediction models of suicide risk are ninety-five per cent ineffective. Researchers found that the assessors, who were experienced mental health professionals, were right in their prediction of suicidal outcome only five per cent of the time. The most deaths by suicide happened in the group of people who had been clinically assessed to be no, low, or moderate risk of suicide. Best-practice suicide prevention is risk-reduction based — identifying risks for that person and removing or reducing them, such as access to medications or firearms — not risk prediction-based, which is more about reassuring the clinician than helping the sufferer. There is a massive difference.

A survivor on the video giving a lived experience viewpoint says that what's really needed is human connection and to know that someone cares; not a 'tick the box', clipboard therapy approach. I reflect that there has been precious little risk-reduction by anyone in my case, and any human connection by health professionals feels sporadic.

No-one else around me seems to know enough about suicide risk, whether prediction or reduction.

I'm so overwhelmed. It's so hard to articulate what I need, yet when I do try, it gets misinterpreted, ignored, or sidelined. The things I think should be blindingly obvious are clearly not obvious to all — why is a crisis mental health team in the capital city of our first-world country taking an old, dangerous, risk prediction approach to suicidality? To feel like I need to be the teacher to those who should be helping me feeds into the very narrative of childhood trauma that brought me here in the first place. The grown-ups are crazy, and they're making things worse when they should know better, but they're the ones in charge.

It's a trap, and I don't know how or if I'll ever get out. I need the Divination spell... but this is real life, there's no dice in my hand, and if there is a spell that might work in calling out for the right kind of help, I don't seem to know it.

WOULD YOU LIKE TO COME THIS WAY?

'...one of the defining elements of a traumatic experience — particularly one that is so traumatic that one dissociates because there is no other way to escape from it — is a complete loss of control and a sense of utter powerlessness. As a result, regaining control is an important aspect of coping with traumatic stress.'

— Dr Bruce Perry: 'The Boy Who was Raised as a Dog'

The second in-person meeting, the day after the crisis team phone call, is nothing at all like the one four days ago with the community mental health team. It's now the school holidays, and my husband is home. I take up his offer to drive me there, but I don't, yet, want him to be a support person.

Half an hour before we are due to head off, he looks at me, puzzled.

'Why do you want to go to these people? I don't like how distressed they're making you.'

Very near the end of my ability to persevere, I feel like there's nothing left to lose by total self-disclosure.

'Who else am I supposed to get help from? I was actively suicidal up until a few weeks ago. The EMDR therapist is away, the GPs know nothing about trauma, and the helplines weren't much better. I have no idea how long it will take to find another therapist. Who do you suggest I go to?'

My husband has no answer while he tries to digest this new piece of information about the recent state of my suicidal symptoms. We head to the car.

I struggle to remember last night's verbal directions. The appointment is somewhere at the local hospital, but not the main, large, modern building. There's something about a car park behind it and the cream-coloured building...? We drive around and think we've found it, until I point out the sign on the end of the building. We're in the staff-only carpark. I get out, walk around to find the hard-to-spot entry for patients. My husband drives around to find where he is allowed to park, and says he'll come back for me. The building looks like a very poor relation of the main hospital, decades older, surrounded by a sea of long wet grass and carparks, with hard-to-spot narrow concrete walkways and next to no signage, acronyms instead of full names on tiny signs by multiple door buzzers. CRS? I think I'm at the right place. I'm greeted at the door and let in.*

'Do you have an appointment? (Yes.) Do you know who it is with? (No.) What's your last name? Have a seat and I'll look you up on the system.'

I'm not a person, just an item on the system. She doesn't even want my first name.

The waiting room is just a narrow awkward hallway, with full glass walls on one side showing a view of some nondescript plants and a courtyard kind of area. There's no one around except down the hallway in some kind of kitchen. I bring out the tennis ball I'd brought to squeeze. I am feeling overwhelmed. I try the positive cognition mantra from my EMDR sessions: 'I can safely get what I need, I can safely get what I need... shit, it worked last time, didn't it? ...I can safely get what I need...'

Two people come into the end of the hallway near me, but not too close, introduce themselves briefly. I reluctantly and slowly get up.

'Would you like to come this way?'

'Not really, but yes,' I reply. I feel rather than see their exchange of looks.

One of the two is my phone caller from yesterday. Do I get plus or minus points in a mental health service for being honest but faintly rude, I wonder?

They show me into a smallish room with a window, a pastel-coloured two-seater minimalist vinyl couch, a similar style pale

---

* Mental health has a long history of being physically pushed as far away as possible from 'normal' people, which continues today.

'*We found that mental health units are usually located on the outskirts of hospitals. Compared with medical wards, they are much further away from the main entrances, the cafes, and other services, such as the radiology and emergency departments. They are also a long way from community services, such as shops, parks and public transport.*'

https://www.otago.ac.nz/news/newsroom/locating-for-recovery-acute-mental-health-units-remain-in-the-shadows. 2 February 2023. See https://rdcu.be/eAQrs for research article.

purple chair, and one other. I'm told to choose my chair. I go for purple. There is a radiator beside me pumping out the heat, so I put my ball in my coat pocket and take the coat off quickly.

They seat themselves, the phone call one is sitting nearest, opposite me.

The other staff member sits off to one side, out of my line of sight, clipboard and pen in hand.

This appointment, unsurprisingly, is mostly disastrous.

'I understand we're here today to make a safety plan with you?' states the woman from yesterday's call. She looks anxious or stressed, as if on eggshells. She doesn't exactly exude the calm, confident but curious and listening ear that I need.

She is about to go on, but I stop the flow. Barely able to speak, stress levels through the roof, on the edge of shutting down, having to force myself to look these health professionals in the eye, angry as hell.

'I think we need to take a step back. I don't feel safe enough with you to make a safety plan.'

The phone caller's eyes bulge just that much bigger.

I go on with difficulty, choked with emotion. I try to explain what it's been like to wait this long, to get such a roller-coaster experience: first one good interaction, then one so bad that the next person believes I should make a complaint: then a simple request for a text before a call is ignored, and that caller simply wanted to dump me into someone else's lap.

The stressed one objects, looking at her companion in alarm: 'No, I intended that we would see you today, that was just another option...'

'Rubbish,' I reply, glaring. 'You never mentioned any meeting in person until I said no to your suggested plan and started getting upset.'

Silence. It's not awkward for me, because I am very, very clear in my head that it's not me in the wrong here.

'It's like being in an abusive relationship, dealing with your service,' I explain.

'One minute I'm being told I really need help, told I'll get help, and the next — it's too long a wait and then I'm told to go elsewhere. I don't feel safe.'

I recognise this pattern: but not from personal experience. Many years ago, I sat in on an introductory session with a friend, in a family violence support organisation. It was explained that women who are abused usually would prefer the physical to the emotional and verbal violence, given a choice: because the physical wounds heal so much faster.* The cycle of abuse that this introductory session described, the 'good' behaviour sucking you in to stay only to experience violence once more, feels much like my terrifying process of reaching out for help that is offered then retracted repeatedly.

There is further discussion about the support I'm asking for — the support I've already talked to two health professionals in this service about, and been promised — and the clear message is, I'm not suited to what they do. They're puzzled and confused by me. I can be given an appointment with a psychiatrist, I can get medication, but what, apparently, I can't get is consistent regular check-ins from someone who understands suicidality, while I find and get settled with a new private therapist. It seems the earlier promises mean nothing.

'So, my husband was right, there isn't any point in coming here because you don't have what I need.'

There is another longish silence, in which I continue to not look at either staff member.

Somehow, we move on from that stuck place, and I realise after

---

* I grew up with the playground chant, 'Sticks and stones may break my bones, but words will never hurt me.' Utter rubbish. Māori have a much more enlightened understanding of the power of words: 'He tao rākau ka taea te karo, he tao kī, titi rawa ki te manawa': 'A wooden spear can be dodged, but a verbal spear pierces the heart.'

a while that they are doing some creative thinking on the fly, trying to cobble together a solution that will work. We land on them helping me find a private psychotherapist: they will phone around and see which of the experienced ones are available. We decide their crisis team will ring me daily, and this is explained in detail: and that I can change it to face to face if needed. They make a lame joke about being a flexible service, 'believe it or not'. Then I'll be passed back to the community mental health team, the ones who assessed me four days ago, who will ring me regularly as needed until I get settled into therapy.

The stressed one says my family really needs to know what's going on with me. They talk about how I can call the crisis team when needed, or the other team on their 24-hour number. I express a reality check of how I'm unlikely to want or be able to do so if I get worse. They suggest I choose a code word that I can tell my husband or a friend as a signal to ring the service on my behalf, and they'd then get in touch. I can't get my head around all that, I don't think it would work for me, but I agree, because I'm over being here. I want out. We finish up just over an hour after starting and I thank them, saying I feel 'a bit less tense'.

Andrew is waiting for me on the hallway chairs. Once in the car I share what happened. At home, he makes me lunch.

It happens to also be our offspring's last day at home before returning to university. She and I do a particularly tricky Technic section of the Lego model we started, 'The Heavenly Realms'. We end in a gale of laughter over how 'challenged' I am — on my turn I'd put a section on one stud too far over, and it took her a bit of deducing to work out what had happened. I rest my head briefly on her shoulder as we laugh wholeheartedly. It's so lovely to laugh.

Being my husband's holidays, we'd discussed going to the movies the next day — *Indiana Jones and the Dial of Destiny*. It's a beautiful sunny day, warm for winter.

Before going, Andrew starts another longish and in-depth conversation. 'What questions do I ask you? Do I have your permission to ask you?' And discussion about our relationship, whether I've been suicidal like this before (no!). It feels like the line of communication is improving along with his practical and emotional support this year.

The small arthouse theatre room has very few for this session, and we'd booked great seats at the back. We miss most of the visuals for the ads and trailers due to some technical glitch or other; there's laughter, and someone next to us says: 'It's a vision-impaired session!' But then the video suddenly appears, the start of a trailer for *Barbie* — an explosion of bright pink.

The Indy movie is everything I need, escapist enough, adventurous enough, Indy enough without being as cringey and cheesy as the originals. The backstory to Indy's in-between years makes sense. And then at the end comes the moment when he's been forced back to his own time against his will — he'd rather stay with Archimedes than go back to his pain in his actual life. His almost-divorced wife turns up, and shows she means to stay. He's injured. She says, 'Does it hurt?' The camera focuses full on his face:

'Everything hurts.'

Harrison Ford delivers the line with enough depth to it to get through to even me, and I tear up.

I almost never, ever cry in movies.

'Me too, Indy, me too,' I say to myself.

My husband contacts the support services that I strongly suggest he use. He bowls up to them in person at their office. The admin person, flummoxed, can't locate a pen and summons up a coloured pencil for him to provide his contact details, explaining that most people just ring and don't come to the office.

My later attempt at a nap is interrupted first by Andrew's phone ringing from the support service, then my daily check-in call from, yes, the stressed-looking one. She exudes the same busy 'I've-got-a-lot-to-do' vibe, more than a 'you are cared for' vibe, but at least now she's not a faceless person and she emphasises that I'll be supported by them, I'll be rung tomorrow, here's the name of one therapist who is available in a month's time, she'll try to find time to ring round others.

Time is clearly in short supply. I am never given any other suggestions of other therapists to try.

I clarify what the phone support will be once I'm handed over (back?) to the community team. She goes on to comment nonchalantly: 'Yes, you'll need support from them until you're settled into therapy. No therapist will touch you without that the way you are now.'

While I think that to be true at this point, it is heart-stopping to be told that so matter-of-factly. She also seems to think I should get in touch with the crisis team not just when I'm having suicidal ideation, but even the next step down — when I'm 'just' catastrophising, just imagining death or disaster rather than wanting it.

I start catastrophising within a few minutes of getting off the phone.

I notice that she's the trigger with all the discussion around handovers and starting a relational kind of therapy and... it's tough. I remind myself to breathe. But I'm not about to call her back about it. If she's a trigger, what's the point?

I demand quite a few hugs from my husband and try to keep busy with sorting laundry into the dryer, but I'm shaky after the call. I mention to him that it's just as well I get handed over to another team in a week or two. I google the therapist mentioned and YouTube for some information on the therapy mode she lists first — one I've not heard of yet.

Andrew's there for me, and tea gets made. I am so very grateful that he's on break.

I contact the suggested psychotherapist, who has no places for another four to six weeks.

I try going to a social event at the local pub and, though tired, find it okay — at least, after sidestepping someone's overly pointed, 'How are you?'

'Literally writing a book about it,' I quip, and the moment passes.

I discover that of all those around the table, I'm the only one to have done a bungy jump, at the birthplace of adventure tourism, Kawarau Bridge, the very first summer this opened.*

Daily calls start coming from the crisis team, more than one without the promised text first. I ring, ask for it to be highlighted on my notes, and get a very understanding person on the line:

'Hell, even I hate calls without being texted first!'

My sleep is interrupted by our heat-seeking cat, and I'm slow out of bed on this second-ever Matariki public holiday.† It feels symbolic of the hope of things to come which I am, only just, believing may be possible.

Ka mahuta a Matariki i te pae, ka mahuta ō tātou tūmanako ki te tau.

When Matariki rises above the horizon, our aspirations rise to the year ahead.

---

* 'The world's first commercial bungy operation opened at the Kawarau Bridge [Queenstown, New Zealand] in November 1988. People couldn't wait to try it, paying $75 to jump.

Visitors would soon flock in from around the world to take part, in what would eventually be recognised at the birth of adventure tourism in New Zealand.'

https://www.bungy.co.nz/about-us/

† 'Matariki is a time for people to gather, honour those who have passed, celebrate the present and look ahead to the future.'

'Matariki made easy: A beginner's guide to the celebrations', 27 June 2024, 1news.co.nz

GHOST FIGHTING

'Traumatic loneliness is probably one of the worst feelings a person can have.'

— Dr Anna Baranowsky: 'Emotional Neglect & Traumatic Loneliness. Ask Dr Anna S.2.E.36', YouTube, 15 October 2015, @What Is PTSD

A few days later I wake at three in the morning, my sinuses a little sore, and get up for milk and paracetamol. Back in bed, feeling just a bit too wide awake. Suddenly I'm slammed by the ghost of the memory I'd chatted over with Andrew so matter-of-factly the day before yesterday.

It was just a conversation in my mid-teens with my dad, how I'd burbled on about myself as teens do, how I'd all but begged for him to say that he approved of me, liked me, was glad that I was born....

I cringe in deepest shame at this memory, this neediness in me. How my father responded, in confusion, that we'd talked more on that one afternoon than his father had ever talked to him in his life. He didn't say that he welcomed my chatting, he didn't respond to my questioning about how he saw me, he didn't say he loved me. He just seemed embarrassed and uncomfortable. And there the memory cuts out. For the time being my last sister had moved out of home, and Dad no longer had to spend quite as much time and energy caring for her. Maybe I hoped that, at last, there was time for me and what I needed, a connection with the only parent who seemed capable of one. Only to be proved utterly, shamefully, wrong.

Now in bed in the quiet darkness, nearly four decades later, I feel small, helpless, trapped, confused. I feel my legs moving as if they want to run away, and yet they feel so stuck at the same time. Every muscle is tense, and the emotional pain is keen enough to make breathing hard. I try breathing exercises. I try telling myself that this is a flashback, mostly emotional, part pure-PTSD as there is the ghost of a memory to hang it on. It's just faint images of my dad's face, and me beside him, as if I'm looking on like an outsider — maybe I dissociated at the time? The emotional pain takes my breath away. Breathe, I tell myself, breathe...

I awaken Andrew, so he hugs me, speaks soothingly, and then drops quickly back to sleep. Not so me. Not for an hour, two hours, maybe a little sleep but three hours later there's still enough pain to make me groan. At one point I take up my phone, scroll a bit, fall asleep with it still in my hand, get jerked awake by a sudden blare of music and the words '... toxic love!' A finger must have slipped onto an Instagram post. Jerked awake, it's much harder to go back to sleep.

I wonder all through this episode when to ring the health team line. Three in the morning seems silly, as that will really wake up Andrew unless I get up on a chilly winter's night. Four o'clock finds me too tired to move; at five, I'm sleepy. In the end I ring towards 8 am, after breakfast in bed and a cup of tea. I'm desperate for a debrief with someone who knows about such stuff.

There's always trepidation with ringing a mental health service now. Who will answer, will they know what to say, will they be of help, or will they add to the misery? This time it sounds like an older woman's voice, with warmth and depth of commiseration.

'I'm not an emergency, I just need to talk,' I say up front.

She brings up my records — I've barely got the word 'flashback' out and she's vehemently commenting how terrible they are. I sigh and relax. She gets it, and we talk for a while. I ponder whether this is a good sign — my brain telling me what needs working on? Or not a good sign, because it feels so bad? She assures me I can ring again today, if need be, she's on till 3 pm, she's glad I'm at the stage of being able to talk about these experiences. She's heard of the suggested psychotherapist — 'Oh, she's good!'

I feel better able to face the day, if still a little shaky.

I stay in bed till mid-morning, finding YouTube videos on flashbacks and posting one on Facebook; receiving heart-melting messages from a few friends. I get up to do some Lego, shower, groceries, lunch, listen to a Radio NZ interview with Lucy Hone on deep grief, nap. I fall asleep to the sound of yet another online therapist's YouTube video.

I'm determined to go into the garden. It's another warmish blue-sky day, and there are ten elephant garlic cloves that have waited two months to be planted. Some weeding, planting, mulching with straw, and I feel good. It's been a long, long while since I've felt that motivated. I see the weeds as another day's good experience to be had, not as some dead weight around my neck. The greens are superbly leafy in the greenhouse, the purple hardenbergia around the pergola column is stunning in only its second season. Somehow, with the massive help of wider family input, our garden has begun to look like the ones in magazines. It has been an astonishing transformation in the past few years. There's so much I could be enjoying.

There's the sound of kindling being chopped. That's our neighbour, and I decide I need to go check if she's turned ninety yet. I haven't been over for a few weeks. I'm instructed to get the gin and tonics ready while she finishes up with the wood. We chat for an hour and a half, till I get the notification that the daily check-in call is about to happen, so I return home.

This time the caller is a youngish-sounding male nurse, and he's lovely to talk to. He's seen the note about this morning, and we talk about it, often with his precursor of 'you don't need to talk about that'. There's a good understanding that repeated talk about something traumatic may be the opposite of helpful, but I'm grateful of a second chance to debrief, as I'm now tired, a bit woozy from the gin, and need to hear his optimism on how we're much better now at these conversations around mental health. I share a little of my sister's psych ward history from the 70s and he agrees, it was pretty nasty back then. We agree I'm okay enough to not need a call tomorrow; he tells me the team will discuss my case on Monday and will ring me then to let me know what they think. I'm thankful it's the third good person to talk to in a row. It makes so much difference.

I wake again at 3 am, but rational enough to quickly tell myself this doesn't mean another flashback is coming. I remember — from where I don't know — that waking around this time may mean your inner child needs attention. Who knows how scientific that is, but if it helps prevent flashbacks, why not?

I search inside for that confused teenage me who reached out to her dad for emotional connection, and didn't get it.

There's almost instantly an image of younger me, preteen at most, sitting on the floor, back against a wall, legs pulled up, head fallen over the knees, arms draped hopelessly over legs. A picture of utter, lonely misery.

'I'm so sorry,' I whisper.

'I'm so sorry there was no one there for you. Sorry you had to wait forty years to get... me.'

I feel clumsy still around younger me. Online therapists in their YouTube videos tell me I'm supposed to listen more, talk less, but this younger me doesn't look like she wants to chat. I think she just wants her misery to be noticed for once. Now it slowly dawns on me that the moment I left home for good, I left her behind, unable to face the pain she carried. I had told myself, if I faced it at all, that I got away from my childhood unscarred, that unlike my sibling, I could have a normal life, be free, and forget. I wouldn't deny that my childhood was unhappy: I simply denied that it had any effect on me as an adult.

I mumble a few more reassuring comments in my head, feel teary, and go to sleep. I don't know if it's present day me, younger me, or both, who started to cry.

Another day, another mental health team worker calls, but doesn't text first. I don't answer. After a short while, a text comes with an apology, then a phone call. It's a mixed conversation with yet another stranger; despite acknowledging she's read in my notes that I don't want medication, she wants to discuss it. I feel the anger rising.

By bedtime I am a bit on the brink of weepiness. The positive energy of being carried along by righteous anger against the world has worn off. I say to Andrew that trauma has damaged me and all my relationships; that I don't have many friends. I've seen a post about the post-trauma damage being worse than the trauma, and it's clearly landing heavily. He goes into overdrive to reassure me how special I am to him, how I'm the best friend he's ever had. This is all stuff he has said regularly, pretty much every day during our thirty-plus years of marriage, and I just didn't realise till now just how much I need that reassurance-love-on-steroids. I can't do normal relationships because I didn't get the relationship building 101 programme that comes from being emotionally close and held by an adult as a child. And it sucks, so badly.

GHOSTBUSTERS

'Our bodies have evolved to be regulated first by other humans, before we can learn to do it for ourselves — and yet beyond childhood this is somehow frowned upon. ...The blockage to this is often in finding other humans who will facilitate this, without us becoming unsafe through revictimisation, exploitation or abandonment...'

— Carolyn Spring: 'Why the Symptoms of Trauma Make Sense', 22 September 2021, www.carolynspring.com

One day I go to the shops, having been texted that the crisis team will ring in an hour, I think I have time to run the errand and duck back. But the call comes in twenty minutes rather than sixty, in the supermarket, so I answer and ask that they stick to what they said, and we agree he'll ring back then.

There's a queue at the checkout, and someone I don't recognise (a mask doesn't help) approaches as if I'm a familiar friend. It's now nine months post-election.

'Do you still feel like you'd want to be on council? (knowing smile) I think of you whenever I hear about them… I voted for you because I liked your structured approach (pause) not all that "Green" stuff…. (pause, and a tone of mild surprise) you're looking good?'

I'm flipped into auto-public figure mode.

'The loss took quite a bit of processing…. It helps me to remember we live in a democracy, not a meritocracy. The most capable candidate isn't always who wins.'

But on the way home, I'm weepy. I don't *think* I had a tense trauma reaction, but there's still a clearly strong reaction. This is not the first such approach by a stranger about the election loss but, thankfully, it is the last.

Curious, I ask my daughter if her flatmate, an election candidate elsewhere in the city, has had members of the public come up to them like this, commiserating months later. 'No,' she says, 'those supporters would be mainly younger, and they wouldn't disturb someone's privacy like that.' Once more I take my hat off to the next generation for their emotional intelligence.

The crisis team member calls, late, apologetic, 'sorry, had something urgent' — 'all good, that's the nature of your job'. We chat; he's a nice guy I've talked to once before, so I relax, but then he enquires whether I've had medication changes (to explain why I'm feeling a bit better?). I talk about hormone treatment, at length, and he finally recalls we talked about this last time. I talk about how this crisis service feels like a speed-dating service and thank him for being one of the few who puts their name on the pre-call text. He asks whether I'm seeing a specialist, an endocrinologist, about hormones. No, I say, just a couple of nurses in an alternative clinic in another town. He's interested but admits he's out of his depth. We agree on me not needing a call till Monday. There'll be a meeting about where my handover is at.

The call is over, but now so is most of the afternoon, and I don't have the energy to go see my neighbour or bake her a birthday cake. I'll aim for tomorrow. Surely a ninetieth is special enough to celebrate for at least a week.

On the weekend my daughter and I go out to support a local sausage sizzle. We google the origins of this Antipodean cultural icon.* She experienced the democracy sausage version while living in Australia. Then we visit the local bookshop with its new collection of Dungeons & Dragons material. The new owner comes over and asks, 'Are you experienced or new adventurers?'

We have a chat about the rising popularity of D&D, the cookbook they're getting in soon. It's such a lovely, normal, affirming moment that a nerdy family pastime is now front and centre in the main aisle of the local bookstore.

I ice my neighbour's birthday cake that I made this morning, chocolate, with yellow M&Ms forming the number 90, and really start to feel I'm pushing the limits. I cook tea — a meal kit service dinner, finding the directions unexpectedly confusing. This is cook-by-numbers; how hard can it be? Andrew helps me, carrying the cake across to our neighbour's. There's a brief exchange with her family member staying with her, and we're invited in, but I'm

---

* See Wikipedia article: https://en.wikipedia.org/wiki/Sausage_sizzle

maxed out. Even a ninety-year-old has more energy than me. We go home to watch TV.

Monday arrives. Now it's two and a half weeks after the first assessment by the community health team, and once more I'm waiting for a phone call that doesn't come.

Andrew asks outright about suicidal thoughts this morning, gratified to hear it had been a few weeks without any.

I watch videos on the therapy mode used by the therapist who I will see and can't get my head around it.

I look up other potential trauma therapy psychotherapists in Wellington. Its mind-busting stuff. The website for the New Zealand Association of Psychotherapists has filters by location or by modality: Conversational Model, Correspondent, Gestalt, Hakomi Mindful Somatic Psychotherapy, Psychodynamic, Psychosynthesis... I've been researching therapy and trauma nonstop for nine months and few if any of these feel familiar to me. What hasn't sunk in, quite yet, is the research that shows it's not the mode of therapy that really counts but the therapeutic relationship itself. I'm still in denial, still in search of the magic that will 'fix' me.*

It's so daunting, and it takes several attempts to make a shortlist. Some therapists have full details and a link to their website; some have just a mobile number; some have a photo, some don't. Do I want a man? Not many of those. I consider, and think no. That doesn't narrow it down much. I know I don't want to pay $500 a session to the guy in the CBD offering a 'bespoke, discreet service'. The cheapest therapists cost around $120; most are more. Someone I know with a relative in the mental health profession

---

* Baier, Allison L., Alexander C. Kline, and Norah C. Feeny. 'Therapeutic Alliance as a Mediator of Change: A Systematic Review and Evaluation of Research.' *Clinical Psychology Review* 82 (2020): 101921 https://doi.org/10.1016/j.cpr.2020.101921.

feeds back that professionals in the field don't always list trauma on their website, because they don't want to be overrun with harrowing sexual abuse cases. That doesn't feel at all helpful when trying to *find* a trauma-experienced therapist.

I email one that does Conversational Model therapy, based on a couple of YouTube videos I've seen about it. She mentions in her reply email that long-term therapy is three years.

THREE YEARS. Holy shit.

That's kinda longer than... I don't know what I had in mind, but not that long. Three years. I don't even want to think how much that will cost, financially. Or what job opportunities may still be there afterwards, if I'm 'fixed' enough for that. I'll be approaching sixty by then!

This is my first big reality check. If I've come across this before in my research, about how long trauma can take to heal, it seems I've been in denial over it.*

I'm having second thoughts about the therapist I've booked, the one recommendation I got from the crisis team. I text to say next week may be too soon, and what would her listed therapy mode do for me anyway? She gets in touch, we have a brief phone chat; she sounds warmer than I expected, says 'I'm not a purist' about her listed modality, that was just all there was available to train in, back in her day. She's old enough to make me wonder how close she is to retirement. We agree I'll text tomorrow to confirm or otherwise about starting next week. I hang up and feel instantly teary, with no idea whether that's a good thing or not. Are they tears of relief? Apprehension? Both? I know, at some point, therapy is going to be hard and painful and... there's not much choice, but I want to feel there is some. And I can tell she senses that clearly, and strongly

---

* 'In trauma therapy, faster isn't necessarily better; it can end up causing more pain and upset...', p. 157 *Traumatized*, by Kati Morton (Hachette Books, 2021).

said it's my choice about when to start, whether I feel grounded enough.

But... grounded. Grounded? How the hell would I know? Do I have to tick this box too, before I even start therapy? Am I now too broken even for therapy, but just not broken enough for the overloaded public system?

I hoover up all the leftovers in the fridge, restart the fire. I feel cold and stiff and weary and lacking focus to do much, but make myself order some Lego parts as that really can't wait too long if I'm going to exhibit at the club's upcoming show.

I'm waiting for a meal kit box to be delivered and a call from the crisis team about their 'decision'. I know which service is more dependable and right on cue as I'm typing this, this very second, the meal box arrives. Still no call from the crisis team.

Crisis? What crisis?

Andrew suggests that I could try his support person for advocacy help. I ring her but just receive a long spiel about the Privacy Act and an explanation that, really, she is Andrew's support, not mine. I start to feel distressed, so I end the call — so quickly, that she rings back. I don't pick up. It's too much.

I message Andrew to ring me at lunchtime.

I've never once asked this of him before.

This morning, while in bed, I have brief thoughts about how to get back my suicide stash I still have at two friends' places, and would only part of it be 'enough'?

I get showered mid-morning, start a fire, have breakfast, then... just sit. I hold a tennis ball but don't even have the energy to toss it from hand to hand for DIY EMDR. This out-of-session bilateral stimulation, including tapping opposite arms and repeating my 'positive cognitions' we'd supposedly established, does not feel like it is working. At all.

I manage to ring the community health team, to ask for info on the decision from their meeting about me. I'm told someone will ring me back.

No-one does.

Instead of a phone call, Andrew unexpectedly arrives home, takes one look at me, and announces he'll be home for the afternoon after going back to pick up things from work. His work colleagues told him to do so. He's also saying he'll take tomorrow off. I realise, yes, I really do need that much help.

It is unheard of for him to take time off.

A meeting with the crisis team is finally set for the next day, Friday, three weeks since my first face-to-face assessment in the public health system, ten weeks since first phoning them for help.

I try directly ringing their office instead of the general team number and ask for a copy of my records, so I have information on hand before the meeting. The lovely person on the phone recognises me from a support call, and remembers our D&D discussion, which she was 'excited' for me about. She reads out bits of the notes — but can't send a copy, because apparently this is a legal process of filling in a form and waiting. Which may take about four weeks.

I'm told that the team decided, over two weeks after my intake interview which promised me urgent help for a serious need, that I can just go to a women's group or use a Health Improvement Practitioner (a new free mental health service at GP practices, using a nurse) for support. They don't see the community mental health team supporting me as a 'good use of resources'.

My distrust of the health system is now total.

I go with hesitation to a first morning games session a friend has set up with a couple of others. We play Bananagrams and then at my suggestion, the card game of choice from my teenage years, 500. We eat homemade savouries, fruit, and the second round of drinks is hot chocolate all the way from Switzerland. It's the most delicious I've ever tasted. The morning flies by. I'm glad I came.

Andrew comes with me that afternoon to the final meeting. At least this time, we know where the building is and where to park.

We're met by an older male and younger female. The man shakes Andrew's hand and offers to shake mine, awkward not just because my hands are wet from sanitising on the way in, but because as I realise hours later, why would I want to shake their hand? It seems an odd thing to do in these post-pandemic times at a health service and implies a level of trust that simply isn't there. I do shake hands, reluctantly.

We go in, are offered a drink, we say no. It's the same room from two and a half weeks ago, just different staff. This time Andrew and I are on the coloured armless couch.

This last meeting goes badly.

At one point the man uses an example about a hypothetical depressive person to illustrate his argument. Andrew leans forward, perturbed — 'You do know the difference between depression and trauma, don't you?' The answer is yes, but it clearly should be no. Even my husband can see that.

The man comments that I've 'had difficulty' with the service I've received. This feels like gaslighting — the difficulty is mainly that their inconsistent service has been bad enough to retraumatise me, but there's no actual acknowledgment of how their actions or systems have been the thing that was wrong — just that *I've* had difficulty. He takes a patronising tone while explaining that suicidal thoughts are common, that I might have them for the rest of my life but that's okay because my therapist (who I haven't started with yet) will help me deal with them. This doesn't exactly come across as at all supportive or helpful, especially from someone who is meeting me for just the first time.

Both staff members insist that the team is there to support me in future. The woman has the grace to look somewhat uncomfortable in saying that.

The man tells us about going to ED if things are really in crisis and I can't keep myself safe.

Funny, I think, isn't that why I came to these people in the first place? Is there even a difference?

After an hour and a half my husband and I walk out with a signed bit of paper, a 'care plan'. It says that they agree not to call me unless I call them. The irony of needing this protection, against a service that is meant to be there to support those in severe need, is profound. Andrew shakes hands, says thank you and appears to smile at them on leaving; I just duck out the door as fast as I can, no farewell.

The piece of paper says I am to ring them myself, after seeing the private therapist. I don't remember agreeing to this. Why would I ring a service I have repeatedly said was retraumatising and who renege on their promises?

Several days later, someone from the crisis team does call despite the promise not to call me proactively, and there is no warning text. I pass the phone to my husband who is as terse and grumpy as I've ever heard him be, reminding the caller there was a signed agreement that the team would not contact me, only that I contact them. My patient notes, when they arrive just a week after being requested, include the caller comment that 'a male answered the phone... he was quite abrupt with me'. No kidding.

My patient notes are a gaslit maze. Over three weeks, there were ten meetings by a 'multi-disciplinary team' or MDT, numbering about eleven or twelve varied health professionals, who made decisions about my (lack of) care while only one or two of them ever met or talked with me. There is conflict and confusions between the crisis part of the service, and the woefully under-resourced community mental health team. A transfer from the crisis team to the regular team is noted multiple times, until suddenly there appears a dissenting voice in the records that care will not be transferred. The last MDT meeting records, 'There were varying opinions within CRS re appropriateness of CMHT referral, but MDT in agreement on balance that private therapy appropriate and not for CMHT at this time.' An earlier note states that the CMHT declined to have me transferred to their care as this was 'not a good use of resources': the final face-to-face meeting with the CRS notes that it was explained to me the reason for decline of transfer was due to the criteria being 'moderate to severe mental health', implying that that assessment had somehow changed along the way — and not something I recall being told either at that meeting or any other time. And rather at odds with the initial face-to-face assessment: in my patient notes sent to my doctor, the nurse recorded: 'Overall, Robyn's presentation is consistent with severe depression with suicidal ideation.' In the patient notes sent to me, the same nurse records: 'She is currently significantly functionally impacted by severe suicidal ideation... an acute assessment is warranted.'

I ring the crisis team some days later to make it clear I want nothing more to do with them. The staff member answering tries to apologise. I'm calmly relating how traumatised the crisis team have left me, but I keep her focused on the practicalities: 'They've ignored written notes before. Could you please emphasise that they are NOT to call me at all now? — thanks.' It's a relief to be off the phone, feeling okay, and in some kind of control.

Andrew says categorically that he never wants me to contact the crisis team again. No disagreement there. He's deeply unimpressed with them, which means a lot from one who almost never criticises people. He says to me, 'It's over.' I'm a bit grumpy with him over his friendly farewell, his shaking hands with them at the end, and we talk that through.

And then about 8.30 pm that night, as we finish watching an

episode from the latest series of *The Brokenwood Mysteries*, he comes over to kiss my forehead, leans over.

I push back, say no, suddenly aware how unsettled I am. I say I'm going to bed. Today has been way too much. The last ten weeks with the public mental health service has been way too much. The inevitable reaction is on its way.

I wake after a seemingly good sleep but am instantly slammed by a wave of pain from yesterday. I don't want to see, hear, or interact in any way with anyone. I'm feeling so wounded again, so utterly, utterly, miserable, bereft, betrayed. Everything is dark; I keep under the covers, keep the blinds down all morning. Andrew makes toast and brings it in, placing it on the bed like you would place food tentatively in the cage of a wounded animal. I eat, but only just. Later Andrew goes off for some baked treats from down the road and shows me the bag; I shake my head.

I'm thinking about how I could get hold of what I need for my suicide plan. I want to die, to escape this pain. I'm so sad for my family that they must see me like this. My daughter sends me a cat photo, but I barely register the positivity this usually brings. After a bit I message an apology for how I am. I message Andrew that I don't want to interact. He replies that he understands.

My friend messages, am I coming to our Lego club day? No. I explain that I can't interact today. Or enjoy anything.

After midday the shadow eases just enough for me to get up, shower, grab some things and retreat down to our large spare room. I shut the door, sit down, and try to relax my breathing. I'm safe here, I'm safe here. I put some MILS plates together for the upcoming club's Brick Show,* but my mind is only partly there.

---

* Modular Integrated Landscaping System. Yes, grown-ups take their play seriously. https://www.abellon.net/MILS/

Around mid-afternoon I see the lounge is empty, and sunny, and I migrate to the window seat.

At four in the afternoon, I've thawed enough to message a rant to my friend about what the last ten weeks dealing with the mental health service has been like. She offers to come round with chocolate bars. Her husband offers to cook us dinner.

She turns up, and I'm finally able to talk.

Andrew's looking a bit shell-shocked. I try hard not to take that personally. It's not till dinner time that I can interact normally with my family.

BACK ON THE THERAPY TRAIL

On the train to my first appointment with the therapist suggested by the mental health team, I unexpectedly meet up with a friend, one of life's fellow travellers from that exclusive club — the kind no-one wants to join, where the condition of entry is deep and painful loss. I gladly chat, feeling safe in such company, a welcome distraction from the appointment ahead. We swap notes on hope and resilience and Lucy Hone; I talk about agency and curiosity some more; they note that hope in the past has been tied to specific outcomes, and that hasn't served them well. It's a freezing cold winter day with a Wellington southerly, but at least not raining. Not for the first time, I sense a deeper bond with those in great grief than almost anyone else.

The therapist's office is a little dark, a reasonable size but that means the chairs are just a tad too far apart; there's a large second heater which I'm warned about and sure enough, it roars into life several times during the appointment. It makes it hard to hear and it's disruptive as she jumps up and down to it many times, asking if it's bothering me. On the third occasion I say yes, turn it off.

At first sight, I don't warm to her. There's not much smile or

BACK ON THE THERAPY TRAIL   151

positivity, much more of an old-school no-nonsense approach. For plus points, she's worked long ago in acute mental health and understands how non-therapeutic it is and how unsuited it would be to support me. She understands attachment issues well; she says I've clearly done a lot of work this year. But she relapses into the jargon of her preferred therapy mode multiple times, not once acknowledging what I said by text and on the phone — this approach doesn't appeal to me. She starts to take notes and talks about boundaries around notetaking; but when I ask about the possibility of doing audio recording, she's clearly a little rattled and it's initially a very strong no.

She then relents a little and wants to know why, but it's too late. I can see despite her saying she works collaboratively, that she wants a large degree of control. I can't bring myself to explain that I'm hopeful this would help me as it helped Stephanie Foo, that I want my own version of Google Docs therapy. I don't yet understand that it's not really about the therapy mode, nor have I seen the research that shows it's the therapeutic relationship that is the most predictive of success[*].

She has a habit of leaning forward and staring me in the eye, and it feels controlling. She goes overtime even as I try to grab my things to go. Then she is sitting at a desk and writing out a paper invoice, the kind that produces three copies. I haven't had one of those in a decade or two.

As a parting shot, she comments I cannot expect to have all that I lacked from childhood restored or made as if the neglect hadn't happened, but that we will work so that I can 'bear my story'. That truly doesn't sound positive enough. I'm no longer looking for miracle quick cures, or even a full cure, but I want more than just 'bearing' life. She's quite clear on how much pain attachment issues create. She offers, as if holding a treat, to explain

---

[*] See Guideline 6, American Psychological Association (2024). 'Guidelines for Working with Adults with Complex Trauma Histories'.

the terms of her preferred therapy mode for me. She asks if I want to confirm for next week and I say yes. I should have said I'll think it over.

I realise afterwards I spent far too much time in the session sharing stuff and far too little interviewing her. I text back, cancelling the next appointment. I need to try someone else. For the first time in a while it's hard to go to sleep: I'm stirred up from sharing too much of the pain without any assistance at dealing with it.

I find, somehow in my internet browsing, that Australia has had a whole website devoted to adult survivors of childhood trauma for *over ten years* now, born out of an organisation supporting childhood sexual abuse but now recognising all the ways children get maltreated. A dedicated helpline, information videos, training for health workers, research. The works. I know we're a small country with limited resources, but ten years behind our nearest neighbour feels like a lot.[*]

In my news feed comes an article that takes months to digest. An international research company releasing its findings for 2022. A thousand New Zealanders aged eighteen or older were surveyed.

One of the questions: 'In the past year, have you ever seriously considered suicide or self-hurt?'

The result is a stunning **one in four.**[†] Twenty-five per cent.

Twenty-five per cent — of *adults*. Half of these experienced it more than once.

The thought is inescapable — this is a public health crisis that no-one wants to talk about. The death by suicide rate is about one in ten thousand per year, in this country. That gets a fair amount of

---

[*] The Blue Knot Foundation: https://blueknot.org.au/about-us/history/
[†] IPSOS Mental Health survey, New Zealand, November 2022. See article – '1 in 4 Kiwis considered suicide or self-harm in past year - survey', 23 November 2022, 1news.co.nz

attention, as it should. But who knew, thinking about suicide is so common? No wonder the health system is overwhelmed. Where is the public education campaign around how to deal with this?

It's literally freezing today. The ice on the deck with the paw prints on it hasn't melted overnight. Andrew fetches me another hot water bottle and checks in whether I've had any suicidal thoughts over the last week. No, I say, but slowly. Other dark thoughts? He asks. Kind of, I say. It is the attachment stuff, the hole. That was yesterday, not as bad as in the past, but still there. 'Can you deal with that with the therapist?' he asks.

'That's why I'm trying to find one,' I snap.

Then I apologise. Then I get feedback that I'm often remote and mysterious. It's okay hearing that but it's a bit baffling. I clearly have no idea how to be open and transparent, which is something I thought I valued, and something I *thought* I did. Clearly not. I don't know myself.

I sit down and tot up how many health folks I've seen in these last ten months. The answer is thirty-five (direct contact, including text, phone, and in person) with an additional ten in the team meeting who declined my transfer of care to the community mental health team. And now, I need to try yet again.

DIAGNOSE OR NOT

'Humanity is too big to hold in one approach or theory... We shouldn't lump trauma survivors into one category. Yes they've had trauma but the reactions to trauma are kind of infinite.'

— Kathy Steele: 'Deirdre Fay and Kathy Steele talk about dissociation and complex PTSD', YouTube, 8 December 2020, @Deirdre Fay

There are many different descriptions of what complex trauma, or C-PTSD, looks like.

This is partly because as a formal diagnosis, it isn't recognised in the United States, despite persistent lobbying by clinicians in the field of trauma, and it has only appeared recently in the World Health Organisation's ICD-11.[*] It's been thirty years since it was first suggested as a trauma disorder category[†]. During those years researchers and practitioners have tried to tease out its differences from 'standard' PTSD, or a myriad of other diagnoses that it can be confused with. It's kind of a moot point for me. I don't need a formal diagnosis since I'm paying for my treatment: I don't have to satisfy an insurance company or the state that I tick a series of arbitrary boxes. One therapist suggested, on my asking, that I may have something called Adjustment Disorder, attachment wounds, trauma. Another says it's developmental trauma.

In the United States the push to have another trauma diagnosis formally recognised other than PTSD has included the suggestion of a diagnosis called Developmental Trauma Disorder. I read the proposed criteria. It doesn't really seem to apply to me. I read the criteria for C-PTSD. That, too, just doesn't seem quite right. I stop caring about the labels, at some point, and look just for whatever seems to fit best.

Paradoxically though, labels do matter. I am part of the Western-model health system: I have little choice. I'm also a human being who badly needs my experience validated. In going over my medical records held by my GP in the aftermath of my complaint, I notice that the 'condition' label attached to my recent visits was... 'Depression'. When I asked why it was Depression and not something like Complex Trauma, I receive an apology.

---

[*] World Health Organization. 2023. ICD-11 (Version 01/2023). World Health Organization.
[†] Judith Herman's ground-breaking *Trauma and Recovery* (New York, Basic Books, 1992).

'We're so sorry, there isn't a category in our computer system for that. We're going to need a system upgrade to add that in.'

WTF?

Almost a year later, I remember this promise and follow it up. No change had been made to my records — but the system had been changed, and the diagnostic label of 'Childhood Trauma' is finally added to my records at my primary healthcare provider. The day this happens, I sit and stare at my laptop screen. There it is, clearly labelled. I feel lighter, brighter: I feel seen, acknowledged, understood. I need the word trauma in my health records, and I'm grateful my medical centre made the effort to accommodate me. But it also feels a bit off, to have to ask, again, and to follow up. Trauma has been studied and researched and written about for decades now. It's far from being just war veterans or survivors of incredibly awful events. I'm glad to be listened to, but I'd rather not be the one who must raise the flag and point out the gaping holes in the system.

With growing awareness of neurodiversity in our family and friends' circle over the last decade, someone exploring the possibility of an autism diagnosis sends me a questionnaire. We talk a bit about how trauma and autism or other neurodiverse symptoms overlap so much. I look online, but therapists on YouTube are only just starting to talk about it. A trauma survivor contacts the CTAD Clinic and is interviewed: the statistics for people with Autism Spectrum Disorder (ASD) also being traumatised is wildly alarming. I bet most adults in my country who manage — after months of waiting — to get an autism diagnosis don't also get screened for childhood (or any) trauma. I'd love to be proved wrong.

Online, I see a post: '12 signs of complex trauma'.* There's a heap of such lists online, but I don't bother to check this one against anything formal, because it's the first one I see where every item resonates, and none feels jarring.

---

* Lilly Hope Lucario: Instagram, April 2022, @healingcomplextraumaptsd

It's a lovely list.

- Emotional flashbacks
- Feeling terminally alone
- Helplessness and toxic shame
- Dissociation
- Persistent sadness & suicidal thoughts
- Repeated search for a rescuer
- Loss of faith
- Profoundly hurt inner child
- Muscle armouring
- Emotion regulation issues
- Deep fear of trusting people
- Hypervigilance about people

By this point I've heard or seen references to all of these, except muscle armouring. What the hell is muscle armouring?

I look that up. Apparently, this is chronic, involuntary bodily tension. It can change the way you feel both psychologically and kinaesthetically, the way you express emotion and perceive both your interior and exterior world and can impede your range of movement. It's not just a crick in the neck or waking up sore from exercise the day before: it's long lasting, because it is your body's physical manifestation of its psychological defences. It's your body bracing itself, and usually, you aren't even aware of it. You could have tightness in the jaw, clench your fists, pressure in the eyes, grinding teeth, restless legs, fidgeting, shallow breathing, numbness, feeling disconnected.*

A friend responds to my Facebook post about this discovery:
'And that's only ONE of the symptoms!'
Exactly.

---

* Sarah Sherwood: 'The Body Tells Your Story: Body Armoring, Part I', September 13, 2016, sarah-sherwood.com

LOSS ETERNAL, LOSS DIVINE

*'Spiritual work doesn't deal with trauma directly.
In fact, spiritual work sometimes can retraumatise people.'*

— Hameed Ali (A.H. Almaas)

A symptom of complex trauma that I don't find much discussion about is the loss of faith.

Some describe this as a loss of ability to see meaning and purpose in life: not necessarily spiritual or religious faith.

I see both versions in me. Faith, if I ever really had it, has truly been lost, along with purpose.

My parents were steadfast churchgoers all their lives, Anglicans, traditional. We attended a very 'high' Anglican church on Auckland's North Shore in the 70s and 80s on our return from Jamaica. The vicar always wore full robes, the choir of very old ladies wore robes, the organist wore a robe. One vicar began a sung chant or plainsong delivery of the liturgy, the set of words said every week in the church service. Everyone thought he was very brave. It was at least a point of difference from the weekly repetition of words whose meaning were never explained.

Those few teenage girls like me who joined the choir briefly received a complaint for daring to wear jeans under our choir robes. The organist was uncomfortable relaying this complaint: a middle-aged woman, younger than the regular choristers, she probably had a teen of her own. She was just happy we were there at all.

I found no connection there to God or anyone else. At my mother's firm 'request' I was confirmed along with a few other young teen girls, all of us in white veils and dresses, presented to the bishop. There was some kind of party at church, and my godmother came, and she gave me a New Zealand history book signed by the author as a present. As far as I could tell, my godmother was the only person I'd call a friend to my mother. The book was mildly interesting. The pre-confirmation classes were meaningless, as was the ceremony. I neither knew nor cared about God: the one time I asked a question of the vicar about infant baptism, I found the answer to be rather poor.

At age fourteen I realised I was old enough to stay home alone. I told a story to my parents that I wanted to stay home to study rather than go to church on Sunday, as this was my School

Certificate year, the first year of important external examinations. I was a good student. Much to my surprise there was no fuss and no argument. I didn't go to any church again until I was nineteen, when university friends convinced me to go to a Baptist youth camp. Baptists don't believe in infant baptism. Maybe that helped tip me over. I felt like I had a Damascus moment, became a Christian, and did the Baptist full immersion style baptism.

For more than thirty years that followed, my husband and I were active churchgoers. I thought I believed, I thought I understood the nature of faith, based on a personal relationship with God. Encouraged by various church leaders, I took courses on preaching. I discovered there was nothing quite like the buzz of being in front of an audience, seeing their faces, delivering a sermon without looking at notes, tackling issues that one pastor confessed to the congregation that he'd rather not.

We left two churches and finally, unexpectedly, after twenty years of being Baptists, found ourselves part of an Anglican church. There were no robes — not at the ten o'clock service, anyway — and much less liturgy than I remembered from childhood. We went because our teens had moved to their youth group, voting with their feet for the church in which it was okay to discuss and support same-sex marriage.

The day after my election loss, a Sunday, I skipped church. Next Sunday, I'm scheduled to preach. My talk is titled 'Knowing God'. I describe what has helped on my own journey. I'm able to sing the songs and say the words of the church service, but everything seems on autopilot. The irony is deep, as all too soon becomes rather clear: I haven't a clue what I'm talking about. I can say the right words, but it isn't my experience. I have no idea who God is. And after some months, I simply don't even care, anymore.

The following Sunday I attempted once more to take part.

Right near the start of every service is a call to worship, with a line said by the service leader, a line or two said in response by the congregation, the words projected up on a big screen.

'We gather to worship, pray, open the scriptures and share in communion,' says the vicar.

'Let us worship in wholeness of heart and mind,' the congregation responds dutifully.

I don't remember seeing these words before. They fail on my lips. I don't get past the first three words.

'Let us wor....'. Wait, what?

'Well, that's not happening!' a super-cynical voice in my head comments.

Wholeness of heart and mind? Hell, no. Not where I'm at.

What on earth is this? Have we had it before?

I ask several people after the service and during the week.

'Is that always the call to worship? Did you notice what it said?'

Apparently, not even the vicar's wife had noticed it.

Liturgy is notorious for often being said on autopilot.

I cannot say a word of the liturgy responses, and I find nothing that resonates in the songs. Often, quite the opposite. There's a contemporary Hillsong lyric that gets the singers to entreat God: 'Rid me of myself...'

I harrumph. By this point I'm fast realising there's not enough of a self in me in the first place. Why should I ask God to take away what little is there? I need more of me, not less.

There's the song that asks,

'Are you broken and hurting within?

Overwhelmed by the weight of your sin?

Jesus is calling...'

Hell, no. *I'm* overwhelmed by what I now understand to be my natural, normal, designed-to-be-this-way trauma response to the 'sin' of others, the collective failings of my parents, my culture, the society I live in, the myth of normal.

It is not normal for creatures like us to leave a mother alone at home with her young child, right when she and they are most vulnerable. It is not normal to have only two adults to rely on for emotional connection. It is not normal to give more priority to things rather than relationships. It is not normal to lock fellow humans up for the crime of being poor and desperate, then make them outcasts and banish them to the other side of the globe, away from everyone and everything they know. It is all of us, collectively, that have gone astray. It is right to be overwhelmed by such a childhood, such a genealogy as mine.

The songs about God being with you in the deepest valleys are the worst.

'He wasn't!' I scream internally. 'That's not what it feels like!'

The one song I like doesn't mention God directly, or sin, for the most part.

'Tuhia ki te rangi
Tuhia ki te whenua
Tuhia ki te ngākau
O ngā tangata katoa...'

(Write it on the sky, write it on the land, write it on the hearts of all people. The song goes on to talk of there being only one aroha, one love, and that is the most important thing of all.)

I try a few times post-collapse to re-engage with church life, through services, training days, small groups. Every time something jars, badly, woundingly.

The only activity that works for me is a monthly pub night where God is rarely mentioned. The EMDR has taken away the extreme bits of my hypervigilance and distrust of people, and I do want some people-contact.

I also just really like a glass of cider now and then.

The very first therapist I'd been taken to stated categorically that choosing to turn away from God now would be to turn away from the very thing that would help me most. At the time that seemed just unfair and a bit annoying. I had no words then, not enough trauma understanding, to describe how very wrong and dangerous that statement was.

Thankfully no other Christian has tried to say the same to me. Maybe some have thought about it. Most seem baffled, completely at a loss. Some have beautiful responses: when a study group leader messaged a link to her favourite worship song, I replied that I'd lost faith and was only just beginning to get back the ability to appreciate the beauty in nature. After her initial reaction she never mentioned anything religious or spiritual again but faithfully sent me photos of beautiful things in her garden, month after month, until not long before she died just over a year later.

My YouTube feed pops up with videos of a Christian psychologist. She has decades of experience working with traumatised clients. I'm wary. So did my first therapist, supposedly; but this one is different. This one spends a lot of time unveiling and denouncing the truth, almost always hidden. The truth that horrific abuse happens in churches and in church homes, by the people children should most be able to trust. She speaks words of faith I can't take in, aimed at therapists and supporters, but she also speaks other words of truth that resonate deeply.

> *Survivors can talk very well about the truths of Scripture but on a lived level it's not real, so they can have the knowledge, but they don't really have the belief and the relationship, because that part of their lives is lived out based on what the trauma taught them...*
>
> *I often find survivors of trauma hold on to their belief because they... are living in self-deceit: it wasn't really abuse, it wasn't really that bad, I know somebody who had it worse.**

---

* Dr Diane Langberg: 'The Spiritual Impact of Sexual Abuse and Other Trauma', YouTube, 29 July 2016, @FOCLOnline

All my adult life, I believed my sister had it 'worse'. Very, very much worse, incomparably worse. She ended up in a psych ward — how much worse can it be? I had walked away from the parental home, went to university, and rarely came back: unconsciously, I believed I could simply leave it all behind me, and just have a happy life.

To discover how deep my own self-deceit went was a shattering experience.

But without that recognition, without that pain of grieving my childhood losses, there is no possible healing from trauma. You can't fix what you don't acknowledge.

Trauma disconnects me from myself, and therefore from others. Relationships of many kinds are difficult, if not impossible, because a true relationship requires foundationally not a faith in the other person's existence, but the lived and felt experience of my own self.

If faith requires a relationship with God, there is no way I can experience it, while I am this traumatised. I am simply too disconnected from myself. Rather than not knowing God, it is my own self I do not know.

In the world of professional healers, some trauma clinicians get overexcited about post-traumatic growth. One series I watch features Dr Gabor Maté and a spiritual leader I have not heard of before, Hameed Ali (A.H. Almaas).* The presenter is a bit giddy with excitement, like a new disciple. He's working with the greatest in the world in this area, those who have gone the deepest, he gushes.

The presenter tries to encourage the purchase of a further series of video teachings from these two greats. These first three free

---

* Trauma & Awakening video series, advertised in Facebook post, 12 September 2021, @Conscious Life. Access to video now unavailable.

videos are just a taster. Unfortunately for him, he has misunderstood and oversold the possibilities.

Hameed carefully explains in the second video:

> 'People who are deeply traumatised, who come to the inner work, to work with the trauma, I usually wouldn't accept them as students. I will send them to a trauma therapist because that's what they need. ... they cannot access the spiritual nature as long as they still haven't dealt with their trauma. And spiritual work doesn't deal with trauma directly. In fact, spiritual work sometimes can retraumatise people...
>
> 'You can't really do spiritual work effectively if you are under the impact of strong trauma.'

This video's title is *How trauma can be a portal to spiritual awakening*.

The irony.

The presenter takes a breath and hastily reframes the discussion with a 'broader definition' of trauma — that 'suffering' would be a better word to use. Suffering, he says, can be a portal to awakening.

Wonderful. All that tells me is that I must get through being traumatised, to a place where I am merely 'suffering'. Then, maybe, the spiritual world will open its doors and enlighten me.

Meanwhile, I'm struggling to get past first base, to find a proper trauma therapist.

I'm not holding my breath.

#5

'It is also important to recognize that the inherent power differential between a psychologist and client can itself hinder the aspiration to facilitate a safe haven.'

— American Psychological Association (2024). 'Guidelines for Working with Adults with Complex Trauma Histories'

The new therapist, the fifth one I've now tried in less than a year, is in a heritage building: old villa-style wooden panel doors, original lift, original intricate mosaic tiling on the hallway floor. There's a lounger-style lie-back chair in her largish office and I'm thankful I'm not directed to sit in that. It looks much too psychoanalytical style, too much like Freud.

She's professional but welcoming, asks if I found getting here okay, and I reply that her directions were great. We sit. She's reading off bits of paper about my rights, expectations of therapy, terms, there's several printed pages that I'm given with an envelope. I ask about audio recording, and it's a no, but not an abrupt no and more about the nature of therapy than about her, which is an improvement on the last therapist. I ask about her trauma and childhood emotional neglect client experience, and what happens if the mode of therapy she uses is not effective? She asks if I do research, I say oh yes, but she still looks pleasantly surprised when I say I followed the link on her website about that therapy mode. She claims effectively to not have had the experience of a client not getting better; but also says she's not perfect and is human. She explains the preferred process for complaints well. She feels old-school strict-therapist-boundary, but I guess that's to be expected especially for a first time.

Afterwards, and for the next day, I'm weepy and my thoughts swirl as much as my emotions. It's the long-haul nature of it which is tough to accept ('six months is a drop in the bucket', she says) — even though my brain knows this to be true, it's tough at this point to have to face it. Somewhere deep inside also wants more warmth and more smiles and more emotion from her, but I also think that's maybe not a great idea really. I don't need more attachment issues; I need to deal with the trailing remainder of those I've already got.

Next time, we are to discuss a safety plan. She's already been onto it — the word suicidal immediately prompts the question 'Do you have a plan?' and I smile, then realising how that looks, and make a lengthy explanation of having had a plan and being actively suicidal, and how that came to an end. I don't say I felt that bad again just yesterday, for the morning.

The therapist smiles and becomes more human when commenting on the lift — I had taken the one flight of stairs. I make a point of taking the heritage lift with its two manually opened-and-closed metal concertina doors. There's no sign on the outside of the lift and it takes a passer-by's explanation to help me work out what to do with them. The ride itself is super smooth and quick, better than some modern lifts. I wonder if there's a metaphor in here somewhere for how this therapy is going to be. I hope so.

The next few days are tough. I'm exhausted again.

One morning I can't make myself get out of bed till afternoon, apart from bathroom trips and to refill the hot water bottle. I try to watch some YouTube videos, but any focus is seeping away fast. I give myself up to the misery once more, several hours in bed with nothing but the darkness in my head for company. I don't want to live. I don't think I'll manage the next Lego club show, or the one after; I'm grumpy about my birthday needing to be celebrated. I've shut the bedroom door, wanting both to hide away and to be found; the only adults left in the house were understandably going about their own day, oblivious. Later my daughter tells me she thought I was out and got a surprise when I emerged after noon in my dressing gown. She said 'Bonjour'... then 'Bonjour?' and I barely managed to grunt 'hello'. I am non-verbal again.

The sunshine had started slanting through the wooden slats on our bedroom window.

Towards the end of the morning I'm catastrophising, thinking about what if the therapist insists my 'safety plan' includes the crisis team's phone number... what if she calls the police on me... what if I get taken to be assessed against my will, and see that patronising man from the crisis team again...? In my imagination, I'm feisty, uncooperative, and able in the moment to insist on my rights, contact a lawyer, to feel angry. All the things I know I struggle so hard to do in the moment.

I realise I've been triggered by talk of a safety plan. I can see once more the stunned and scared look on the face of the social worker at the crisis team. I need to find a different name for the plan. Maybe... the Anti-Suicide Plan? The Keep Robyn Alive Plan?

I long for Andrew to come home and be understanding, and he does. There's a long list of chores that he needs to do because I can't — emptying food scraps, rat poison in the attic, swapping cars around to charge his EV, getting in kindling, starting a fire, making me a cup of tea. He's tired but doesn't let on; he asks what I need ('Shall I keep you company? Do you want to talk? Watch TV together?').

To say the second session the following week with this therapist was a shock would be a grievous understatement.

We take our seats, look at each other, and she begins.

'I've been thinking...' says the therapist, and I brighten up momentarily, 'that I have a gut feeling I can't be helpful to you. There won't be a charge for today. I wanted to tell you in person.'

I stare.

A few days later, I write my second complaint of the year.

I wish to make a formal complaint regarding Ms X, a registered psychotherapist...

After approaching Ms X via email, we had a first meeting on Monday 21st August for approximately one hour.

We made a further appointment for the following Monday. It was agreed that this session would cover a safety plan. It was agreed that I was a private client, not covered by ACC.

I noted to her that sometimes it takes me a while to understand how I feel, and said I would be in touch should I not wish to proceed with therapy with her before that appointment. Since I decided to proceed, I made no contact. There was no indication by her either in her otherwise excellent written material, prior email, or during this first session, that she would choose not to proceed or what such a process would look like.

Ms X was aware I had issues with suicidality over the last ten months. At the first appointment she asked whether I had a plan, and I discussed the nature of my suicidality including a period of several weeks of active planning and gathering means.

She was also aware that I had trauma from childhood emotional neglect, and previous treatment by an EMDR practitioner but no other talk therapy.

I discussed how the incompetence or failure to care for me by professionals or those in a caring role is a trauma-triggering event for me.

I came to our scheduled appointment on Monday 28th August fully expecting to discuss a safety plan to proceed with therapy.

Instead, Ms X announced that she had been thinking and decided that she could not be of help to me. This was a 'gut feeling' which she could not dismiss, and she wished to tell me in person, and that there would be no charge for the session.

This came as a huge shock. I asked for further details as to why but was again just told it was a 'gut feeling'.

I expressed that I didn't see this coming, but that I appreciated her saying it in person. I showed visible signs of distress (head into hand, weepy). My jaw had literally dropped. Signs of shock would have been obvious.

I asked if she could recommend any other therapists competent to deal with trauma.

She bluntly replied no, all therapists she knew had no vacancies due to COVID increasing demand for services. She made no other suggestions at all as to where I could seek help.

She suggested that I go to a cafe down the road, have a hot drink, and 'sit with this feeling'.

I was in such shock I made conversation about the cafe in question, thanked her, then left the room in a hurry as I felt overwhelmed and unsafe, and it was very clear that she had no further comments or help to provide.

This exchange lasted 10 minutes or less.

Once I had left the building, a trauma reaction was in full force. I was almost hyperventilating, shaky, barely able to take in my surroundings, and feeling hopeless about what to do next. Thankfully I was able to ring the family member who had dropped me off, to come back (a twenty-minute drive) and pick me up. I had been expecting to take the train home, but I did not feel able. I felt overwhelmed and abandoned, just as I had done in childhood.

My muscles were very tense and ached for the rest of the day, to the point where I deemed it necessary to take a sleeping pill that night, my first ever. I do not take any medication lightly and it is always carefully researched and, usually, a last resort.

Even by my currently reduced standards, the impact on my ability to function was significant.

I respect a practitioner's right, indeed obligation, not to proceed with treatment if they believe they cannot assist the client. This is not the basis for my complaint.

My complaint is that her announcement of not wishing to proceed with me breached the Psychotherapists Board policy and guidelines, by leaving me traumatised and without taking reasonable steps to provide for my safety.

I believe she should have taken several simple steps to ensure my safety in communicating her decision not to proceed.

These steps should have included contact before the appointment indicating that I should if at all possible bring a support person to wait for me.

It should also have included suggestions on how to seek alternative professional help, such as considering a return to my EMDR provider, direction to a website such as TalkingWorks *(which I was not aware of until a friend showed me), or to suggest considering online therapy.*

I believe she had enough information to realise that her announcement would come as a shock, would be perceived by me as abandonment, would be a traumatic experience, and that I would require support to be safe.

I believe her conduct amounted to serious risk of harm as referenced on the website of the Psychotherapists Board.

Writing the complaint, I feel shaky. I'm able to keep focused and keep going, which is pleasing. But I feel like I'm having to put more effort into evaluating, finding, and then complaining about professional support, than getting any.

The day after writing the complaint, I sleep well: but on waking, I try to go about the day, give up by late morning and retreat to the bedroom. I lie on the bed in overwhelming pain, unable to even watch YouTube or respond to messages. I just want to die. Again.

I search up overdosing on household meds. I search up sleeping tablets. I found that there are some indications even the non-benzo type I took one of can lead to suicidal thoughts. Wow. Wasn't told that by the GP.

Andrew and I have an upfront conversation. He sees my negative bias; I say, that's what kept me safe as a kid — hypervigilant scanning. He says he'll continue to keep showing me unconditional love. I don't have to do anything for it, just exist. The smallest smile or positive response from me gets a gleam of joy from him, but he insists that I don't have to reply to his 'I love you', I don't have to respond, it's okay to not be okay.

Hearing these words out loud is very, very healing.

I fall ill for a week with a virus, miserable, sick, and suicidal. In a good moment I ask my husband to remove something else from our house that could be dangerous. I've missed the last day of my first

Brick show in five years: my family and a friend need to spend an hour and a half packing down my dining-table size exhibit. I've tried for the first time in months to do something for me, something fun, and it has failed.

Andrew goes all out over the fortnight of school holidays to look after me. Breakfast in bed, making me lunch, cooking dinners, taking over tasks like remembering the recycling. With lots of acknowledgements, encouragement, and checking in. It's amazing. It's so different from what I got as a kid.

I go to the doctor in case there's any infection to deal with, and I'm seen by a locum. The locum GP finds no bacterial infection and offers codeine as a cough suppressant. Once home and thinking more clearly, I research. Codeine has been shown not to work for coughs. It's not standard or good practice any more in this situation. It is addictive even in small amounts and could be dangerous in other ways.

I message my new doctor to ask that a red flag be put on my file that any meds to be prescribed be assessed for suicide risk first. My doctor confesses to being 'disappointed' given my history that I was prescribed codeine and adds alerts to my file as asked.

Idle in recovery, I'm browsing online and find a kitchen cabinet supplier that I've been keen on is having a liquidation sale. Solid oak at sixty per cent off? Unbelievable! I message a family member, who excitedly says he's coming round in two hours to discuss. It feels like a rare ray of light in a very dark year. We'd had a nearly six-figure quote for our proposed kitchen and dining renovation, the week after the election loss. With all my income, and future income prospects, just disappeared, it didn't seem like the time. Now with the offer of family help, the project is on again.

I spend an hour helping a volunteer from the community garden access its Google account. I'm happy to do so, but I am tired. And I am clear to myself — there isn't a 'going back' to the garden. I'm not ready for volunteer work yet, for giving of myself. There's still not enough of me to give. And the garden wasn't enough to save my mental health, after all.

With some mental energy returning, I tackle some odd transactions on our credit card that I first noticed five months ago, that I didn't have the energy to follow up as I usually would. They're from Andrew's card and he doesn't recognise them. I ring the bank. We've been scammed. We get only three months' worth of payments back. The other $300 is unrecoverable. We agree that we both need to take responsibility for checking our card statement every month, not just me.

Counting the cost of trauma just got a bit too literal, for my liking.

#6

'It's one thing to feel our own feelings on our own sitting on our sofa... it's such a different thing to feel our feelings in front of another person...it's infinitely more scary, vulnerable... that's a huge part of why therapy works.'

— Forrest Hanson: 'Cognitive Bypassing: How to Get Out of Your Head' | *Being Well* podcast, YouTube, 10 April 2023, @Forrest Hanson

Somehow, miraculously, I feel just well enough to try contacting another therapist. And she has vacancies. At the end of October, just over one year post-election, we talk briefly on the phone. She seems to understand complex trauma. I tell her what happened with the last therapist. She pauses.

'I'm surprised you're coming back for more therapy after that.'

The kitchen cabinets get delivered the day before, so a friend and I spend two hours that day unboxing them, checking if the glass doors are okay. The delivery had taken two weeks longer than expected. By this time, I feel vividly convinced I'm a victim of fraud and it is too good to be true. It's so strong and so odd, so close to a delusion, so unsettling, that any enjoyment of the delivery is impossible for days to come. I'm numbed out.

My first session with the new therapist is on 31 October. I aim to arrive five minutes early but take a wrong turn because my phone is playing up and get there two minutes late.

Going to psychotherapy is unlike any other health appointment. The time slot is sacred. You won't be let in early; you won't be made to wait; you can't go overtime. The process of arriving and leaving takes on huge significance.

Her office, an open-plan area with a large window, has a view of trees on the steep hillside framing the harbour. It's got white walls, spacious because there's just a couch and her chair, and a pot plant or two, a couple of side tables. She says her last office felt too claustrophobic. Having been in several like that by now, I think yes, it's probably worth paying more for a better space.

She asks if I want a drink, she fetches me water. We sit.

'I know it is difficult to come to therapy...' she starts.

I interrupt.

'Just for context, you're the sixth therapist I've seen in the last year.'

There's a brief pause while she visibly does a reset, then she goes on with further comments.

I ask, 'What about timekeeping?' and quickly she responds: 'That's my job.'

I explain that I've had health appointments before that went overtime without asking me and then charging me for the extra.

I feel more relaxed than with most therapists initially. There's not quite the same rush to get all the bad stuff out, to convince her that I need help. I've already decided to try to start with the positives and say what's been built up or strengthened over the last year — my marriage, grown-up kids, friend, supporter, financial security. I forget the hormone clinic initially but come back to that later, and she's even heard of and dealt with them previously: a rarity among health professionals.

I talk of my EMDR experience, and that offering of the community mental health team number as a backup, and how badly that went.

'Oh yes, they would have made things worse,' she says.

I reply by saying that using the word suicide usually makes therapists a bit nervous.

She furrows her brow momentarily: 'But that's our job to deal with such things.'

Her face lights up many times during our fifty minutes. When I describe the results of my leadership coaching, when we go through the list of things I DON'T have wrong with me.

'Do you have problems with food? Other addictions? Substances?'

'No.'

To short circuit a long list I offer, 'I also don't self-harm.'

I raise the point that I don't have a lack of self-worth.

Her face lights up again — 'That's great' — but this somehow makes me annoyed.

I'm still here, in therapy, still having endured a year of on and off suicidality. How can it really be great? But on reflection she didn't disagree with me, as the first two therapists bluntly did. And she's quite overwhelmingly positive about what the outcome may be for me, the possibility of finally using all that untapped potential, the chance for 'another go'.

My stomach clenches ever so slightly and my eyes widen, and on the way home I'm weepy. At home, I feel small and scared. I don't know if I can handle this much hope right now. I'll need to tell her so, next time. Because, scarily, I feel that there will be a next time, and quite possibly many more next times. She's been focused, but relaxed and low key and gives me plenty of space and time to make up my mind about booking the next session, reassuring that the next session won't commit me to any further. That with even long-term therapy I could duck in and out as needed, that I may need to go back for more EMDR, that EMDR was kind of diving in the deep end, and it won't happen like that here. She talks about pacing, and I say I don't think I'm any good at that. 'That's my job,' she says.

'You may not feel it, but you'll be tired after this. I hope you have a quiet day ahead?'

'I'll do some gardening, I think.' In my head I say, what day isn't quiet? There's so little I've been able to do over this last year, even my busiest of days is 'quiet'.

At home, I reply to a message from a friend. I feel unable to do anything much. She offers to come round later, I say yes. She's enthusiastic about my report on the therapist.

'This one sounds so good compared to the others!'

To be accurate, that's rather a low bar.

Andrew checks in and is also happy with the positive news. He tells me the stockpiled pills I gave him aren't around anymore, he has them safe. We discuss that these aren't really the 'stockpiled' ones, that he should get rid of them anyway.

'Are there any more pills that I should know about? — I'm sorry, I'm sorry for asking...'

I cut his apology short with a glare.

'Of course you can ask, that's what keeps me safe, that's what NO-ONE ELSE has been asking,' I say, with feeling.

We go to a play in town, the first outing in ages, *The Importance of Being Earnest*. I'm a bit excited to be going back to live theatre. But then tiredness, tearfulness, not enough safe human contact during the day; a feeling of disconnect whenever my husband is around but not totally focused on me; the overwhelm of too many people around me at the show, too many possible interactions. Too close to the stage, actors looking you right in the eye. And while I'd remembered some of Wilde's one-liners from forty years ago reading the play at school... I'd forgotten one that hits badly.

'All women become like their mothers. That is their tragedy. No man does. That's his.'

I know it's not actually true. Andrew tells me it's not true. My own grown-up kids have told me it's not true, over and over and over again. I'm not like my mother. But it's still my greatest fear, that I might be, even momentarily. I have half her genes, and she had the main role in raising me, so what's stopping me becoming like her? What's stopping me from talking in monologues, overwhelming her hearers? From being narcissistic? From being someone that no one wants to be around. From being toxic?

I grasp at another Wilde quote.

'The truth is rarely pure and never simple.'

The week after starting with therapist number six, I fly to Auckland, the first time in over a year.

It's barely an hour's flight. I'm unsure if I have the energy to do this trip, but I want to try. The last time was to visit my sister in her care home, having another 'she-might-be-dying' health episode. That trip was two months before the election, another stress in an already stressful year. I'd talked to the new therapist about it, watched her eyes widen, heard her say how stressful it had all been

— and all I'd thought was, that was just one year. Wait till you hear the rest.

So, a trip to Auckland, first solo trip anywhere this year, a testing of my strength.

I had chosen a window seat. Two men sit in the middle and aisle seats. The plane is delayed by technical difficulties with the baggage handling. At one point half the planeload of passengers is asked to disembark, but our row stays. And by now I'm beginning to realise that there's something off about the man sitting next to me: he's wasted. I don't smell alcohol. Drugs? One minute he's being conversational. The next, he's falling asleep, at ten in the morning, his head dropping onto my shoulder.

'Hey!' I say loudly, looking across to the well-dressed man in the aisle seat, pleading for backup. The wasted man wakes up. He struggles to stay upright. The other man gives him a brief pep talk — 'Mate, you've got to stay awake! Big night?' The wasted man's head droops onto the aisle-man's shoulder. Aisle-man and I exchange grimaces: I put on headphones, squeeze as close to the window as possible, prod the middle guy awake whenever needed, and try to take deep breaths. I don't want to get triggered. This trip has barely begun.

The first, morning visit to Liz is okay, but returning to see her lying down in the afternoon, she looks terrible. She is unusually negative and upset by someone else not in their right mind. It's hard to tell if this is a delusion. There's every possibility of that kind of conversation, in a rest home. But even so, this doesn't seem like the Liz I know. I've done this trip, stayed in this friend's house, so many times. But now it feels unreal. Except the smell of urine that hits my nose on walking in the door of the rest home.

That's all too real.

The next day is Liz's seventieth birthday. Just ten minutes into my visit she's whisked away for a care procedure. Then a staff member comes to fetch me, to be with her in the courtyard, and then maybe half an hour later staff are back again, to do the procedure, and Liz is making the distressed noises an animal or small child does. It's not a distressing procedure for most people, but it is for her. I sense she's not screaming the place down like the last time they tried it, as they told me she did, because I'm there. I reach out my hand to place on her arm for reassurance. Her body is totally rigid with tension.

The staff do what they can, say they'd like to do a little more, they 'don't want to keep traumatising her', and my mind spirals. This is so, so horrible. I don't want to live. I don't want to bear witness to this kind of pain anymore. Especially not now I believe it was caused, for her as for me, by childhood trauma, at least in large part — with a dollop of genetic predisposition and intergenerational trauma probably added in the mix: there's a fair amount of evidence that childhood trauma can lead to a whole range of autoimmune disorders, including — in fact especially — the one Liz has.*

I'm so exhausted I lie down and doze for nearly two hours that afternoon, before getting ready to wait for the shuttle to the airport.

---

* Dr Gabor Maté, in the *The Myth of Normal*, writes at length about the increased incidence of autoimmune diseases in overly compliant, often female, and usually traumatised patients.

TRUST

'Being known by another person is just as vital to life as listening to a baby's cries to figure out what they need and that the first step in helping people overcome childhood trauma is to help them feel known at every level of their being again.'

— Dr Jacob Ham: 'The Nurturance of Being Known', YouTube, 8 July 2017, @Jacob Ham

The morning of my second session with the newest therapist, I partially wake in the early hours from a nightmare about me being kidnapped.

I say to Andrew and our daughter that lots of health professionals can seem fine the first time — it's the second time they start saying what they are really thinking.

The appointment is a different time, as I won't get a settled regular slot until I've agreed to continue, and one becomes available — likely next year. There's rush-hour traffic but much, much less than pre-pandemic.

The view out her office window is stunning, a harbour view framed by a large pōhutukawa tree, on a sunny, blue-sky day with a slight chill that's going away. There's a brief awkward pause as she sits, and I bring myself with an effort to look her in the eye.

'So, how does it feel to be here today?'

Oof. I laugh, repeat what I said to my family.

'So, there's no trust there.' It's a statement, not a question, calmly made.

She explores in more detail what 'went wrong' with other therapists — 'I don't want to repeat their mistakes.' She remembers I told her she's the sixth one I've seen in a year.

She looks closely at me, concerned.

'You look tired and stressed...'

Yes. I report the nightmare, mention the visit to my sister in Auckland. She waits, expectantly, not saying the usual mantra of society ('that must have been nice to see her!') because she clearly sees what I'm not saying — it wasn't a fun visit. I describe that in more detail, I add on about the memory of calling an ambulance for her when I was about nine. She shifts in her seat, makes a face, and exhales loudly. She's telling me what I know in my head but can't quite recognise — that this was really, really tough for a kid so young.

She asks what things are like now, she remembers it's been nearly two months since the last really bad day.

'What do your bad days look like? Your more usual days?'

We explore suicidality. She's fine with just my close support team of family and friends. She really understands that the public system usually does more harm than good, these days.

I forget to tell her what a mental health team social worker told me (after just one face-to-face meeting and one phone call), that no therapist would touch me now I was suicidal, without support like theirs. While also trying to fob me off to a charity organisation. Yet here I am, with a therapist who doesn't find this a problem.

'Robyn, you haven't had any repair in the therapeutic relationships you've had, you haven't had enough sitting with the pain, enough witnessing of that, enough attunement to your needs…'

I'm unable to answer except to nod and look sadly but briefly into her eyes. I sense I'm going to be weepy again the rest of the day because of this one thing, let alone the rest we talk about.

She gives a five-minute warning — anything else I want to raise? I mention the one thing that resonated both badly and well last time — her comment of my getting a second chance at being able to have a career role, something worthwhile. I explain that I'm not ready to look to the future or to hold that kind of hope; it's too painful. She apologises.

'My job is to think such thoughts, but not to say them out loud; to "hold" them, and you, in a safe container. Would you like to make a next appointment now? Or later if you're not ready?'

This time I say, yes please, let's make one now. Because for the first time, I finally, finally, feel that someone who might possibly be of help is here for me, listening to me, competent, able to repair mistakes, and understands. Someone who sees how much pain there is even though I haven't yet shut down or cried. No matter how many times she says this approach is gentler than what's gone before, the brute reality is still there. The pain needs facing and witnessing. Therapy is going to be hard work in ways I can yet barely comprehend.

. . .

In the third week of psychotherapy, I have two more nightmares, but far less weepiness.

This week is a late afternoon appointment. The timing does not work well for me.

I sleep badly, going over and over what we said and what I would say next, reliving my entire life. In the early morning hours, I try the container exercise with my friendly dragon. It takes a few goes but I do get sleep. Not enough, but some. I've also noticed some involuntary body twitches and shakes again in the last day or so.

I'd woken in the morning to the most horrific nightmare. In my dream, one of my children was a baby again, and I'm putting her to sleep, arms outstretched... and somehow manage to knock her head off like a Barbie doll. She's dead; there's no blood but it's so shocking and grotesque, and in my sleep, I'm screaming and screaming in primal pain of hurting (killing!) my beloved child.

The therapist did ask whether I write down my dreams, so I suppose this would be a good start? I have never screamed like that in a dream before. I have nightmares about being trapped in my house as it gets washed away in a flood, about being kidnapped, about failing as a parent, about a man physically assaulting a boy and me unable to stop him. All these are unusual. Usually, my bad dreams are about buying a bad house (we're still in the same house we bought over thirty years ago, with no intention of moving) or being stuck in a hideously dysfunctional public toilet (were the toilets of my schooldays really that bad?).

We talk about where I'm at now on the suicidal continuum, and I say, a step down from it — catastrophising happens a couple of times a week.

'Are these thoughts like, I'm worthless?' she asks.

'NO,' I reply vehemently, 'never, it's always about death or serious harm to me or someone close to me. There's not criticism of myself, it's not low self-worth, I don't have that.'

'That sounds more like anxiety.'

I take a while to digest that. Somehow it feels weak to admit to being chronically anxious. Hypervigilant sounds sooo much... sexier?

We agree to meet next week, and to talk over a permanent client slot.

'So, you think you can help me? I … I guess I'm half-expecting to be dumped,' I comment, a bit sheepishly.

'I'm not in the habit of dumping my clients,' she says in a tone of firm distaste.

She looks deeply unimpressed at the reminder of my previous therapist experiences.

We talk a lot about my life, other times symptoms have occurred, my relationship with Andrew and our grown-up kids, how the public mental health service being so bad led to much better communication around suicidality with Andrew.

'There was a seven-week wait to see the mental health team,' I casually mention.

She interrupts. 'Seven weeks? While you were suicidal?… I would expect that kind of wait for an ADHD assessment!' We reaffirm that their service is of no use to me.

'I went to them because I needed someone to check in on my suicidality regularly.'

'Do you give me permission to ask that here?'

'Absolutely.'

'We'll make it part of our structure.'

Several times in talking about my adult life she comments, 'that would be pretty stressful' which makes me pull up short, inside. We're barely started. There's so much more even as an adult that has been stressful. But there's also been good stuff. Doesn't everyone have stressful things? Are we going to talk about every single stressful thing in my life?

I have a long, long list of questions for next time.

Next week, five minutes before going to therapy, a response about my complaint from the Psychotherapists Board arrives by email. Apparently, there were no breaches of ethical standards or clinical competencies in being unceremoniously dumped by the last therapist. Just some 'minor procedural matters'. No details. Case closed.

I arrive, shaking, at therapy. I read out the response.

She focuses on how I'm feeling. The classic, 'How do you feel about that?'

'All feelings are welcome here,' she emphasises. 'What had you hoped the response would be? What will you do next?'

She makes little other comment and moves to questions about the time prior to the election. When I list off the things that happened in the two years before that, her eyes widen. Learning how to be chair of an elected body, pandemic a few months later, two offspring living overseas unable to be visited, suicides impacting the community, dealing with bullying behaviour, sudden perimenopausal haemorrhaging, surgery for that, cataract surgery, catching COVID three months before the election, my siblings' health crises... Well, the whole world had stuff going on. I was no exception.

'I think your reaction to the election loss was a narcissistic collapse,' she pauses and then says hastily — 'I'm not calling *you* a narcissist: we all have an ego, and your whole sense of self appears so tied to what you do, that being forestalled from fulfilling that feels like life isn't worth living — your "self" collapses.' I mentally add yet another new psychological term to my internal dictionary: narcissistic collapse. But collapse — yes, that describes it well.

We agree to make ad hoc times till the year end, and she takes my preferences for a regular time slot in the new year.

· · ·

The next day, I drive a couple of hours north with a friend for a Brick Show run by my club. I'm nervous. I haven't driven out of town for months, nothing that I've hoped to do this year has worked out, and instead of the excitement there could be, there's mainly just a sense of quiet dread. The drive up is uneventful, the unload and set-up are tiring but goes well. Mine takes the two of us about two hours, a dining-table size 20,000-plus piece display combining major Asian-themed sets.

Back at the motel we discover the toilet is jammed so close to the vanity that your knees go under the wall-hung unit, that they use a lot of awful air freshener, and saggy inner-sprung beds are not great when you're used to the reliable firmness of slats.

At 2 am I wake, too hot — the duvets and covers are synthetic and don't breathe.

At 4 am I awake with lower back pain; and I panic.

I collapse, inside.

It's the end, I can't do the show, I can't plan on doing anything, nothing will ever work out, how will I get home, what if paracetamol doesn't stop the pain? I feel alone in the dark, helpless and hopeless, and for a brief while, I just want to die. Everything is just too hard.

Waking my friend feels out of the question, even though her bed is just a couple of arm-lengths away. Awake again a few hours later, I'm groggy with tiredness and post-trauma reaction fatigue, but there's no back pain. Just the shame of yet another meltdown, yet another round of pathetic weakness.

Over breakfast my friend shares her lack of sleep, so I mention mine and allude to not being 'good' in the night. She looks up, concerned.

'Is that something talking about will help, or not?'

I briefly describe it, catastrophising, and hopelessness. She's familiar with this, she understands. We get on with the day and reflect later, we're both so glad I kept going and did the show. But I couldn't have done it without a friend who understood.

And the show itself... our club has grown a lot in eight years, and now the venues we need are the size of indoor sports centre stadiums, with over 120 exhibitors. All the wonderful, amazing reactions from the crowd: kids whose faces light up because I have their favourite Ninjago characters in my display, grown-ups who love the sight lines and design elements and sense of discovery. On the second day one show visitor discusses the logistics of getting it here, and thanks me sincerely for the effort I made.

It's incredibly satisfying. There are chats with a whole range of other exhibitors — past friends, new faces, old, young, lots of neurodiverse folk. By the end of two days, I'm just amazed. It worked. I survived, I loved it, we even managed an evening walk around a huge rose garden and eating out at a great Indian restaurant. I have few decisions to make and no one I feel responsible for, no expectations, and I come home feeling like I've found something important again in myself. I find a Brené Brown quote about creativity* and post it up with a few close-ups of my Lego show display.

The evening of arriving home from the show is my last night for taking out a contact lens, my last remaining one. I had cataract surgery a few months before the election in one eye, and now the other also needs doing.

I have been massively myopic since late primary school: at age ten there was a check-up at school where I couldn't read the top line of an eye chart — the one with only one, very large letter. I thought all eye charts started with 'E'. This one had an 'F'. I couldn't tell. I'd been hiding my poor sight for a year or two, not

---

* 'The only unique contribution that we will ever make in this world will be born of our creativity. If we want to make meaning, we need to make art. Cook, write, draw, doodle, paint, scrapbook, take pictures, collage, knit, rebuild an engine, sculpt, dance, decorate, act, sing — it doesn't matter.

As long as we're creating, we're cultivating meaning.'

Brené Brown, *The Gifts of Imperfection: Let Go of Who You Think You're Supposed to Be and Embrace Who You Are.*

wanting the stigma of wearing glasses. The shame of having such poor eyesight hit hard, but I only wore glasses for six months until the optometrist suggested contact lenses as my eyesight was getting worse. Very few people wore contact lenses in late 1970s New Zealand. I was a novelty for years.

There's the sense that here's something else that might go right this year.

Cataract surgery day involves a long, long wait beforehand and an unnerving talk with a possibly anti-vax medical person. Just because I spoke about challenging the medical establishment doesn't mean I am willing to go there!

I feel much more vulnerable during the operation than last year, much more tense. I silently repeat to myself that I'm in the hands of a top eye surgeon, that I'm being well looked after, just breathe, just find something else to think about. All the while there's a weird kaleidoscope of light going on in my eye and time seems drawn out, stretched, while I desperately focus on not moving, not a sneeze, not a twitch. Low resilience, or just more aware of how I feel now? Something to ask the therapist. Was I better at this last year because I dissociated so well?

ANCIENT DRAGONS

'What is at the core of our mental health is not an individualistic pursuit, but it is the depth and the connection that we make with other people... that no other experience can provide.'

— Esther Perel: Instagram, 2 May 2024, @estherperelofficial

Another therapy appointment.

She states that in our therapeutic relationship there will inevitably be some transference, some more of the attachment wound as I've experienced before with someone being a support.

I immediately react.

'God, not as bad as that, I hope!'

I don't want that kind of pain again in my life. That's the void, the unbearable void. That's what came from having someone with listening skills, who made me feel seen, who blew open the hole in my soul, for whom I had the humiliating, shameful experience of feeling all the emotional reliance of a toddler, to whom I would alternate between being an emotional cling-on and being an eruption of private anger: the push-pull, can't-live-with-or-without you inability to trust that can lead the unlucky to the modern hysteria diagnosis of borderline personality disorder.*

'No,' she reassures, 'no, I focus on stabilisation for you first. What are your goals for therapy? Your expectations? I know you said last time you're not ready to hope for future leadership roles.'

'I want... more resilience ... more ability to take in the good and not be so fearful of the bad. Specific goals — I want to write, I want to finish the book I started about my experience, maybe do some advocacy work.'

I'm on the brink of tears most of the way home. Maybe it's just the realisation that the 'easy' part of therapy is over, the introductions, the circling round and scoping each other out. From now on, we're in for the tougher stuff.

Over the week I feel more childlike again, more helpless, more vulnerable. It's not that I don't want to talk about things with the therapist. It's more that I don't want to feel so bad again, I am

---

* Natalie Dorfman and Joel Michael Reynolds, 'The New Hysteria: Borderline Personality Disorder and Epistemic Injustice', *IJFAB: International Journal of Feminist Approaches to Bioethics* 16, no. 2 (1 October 2023): 162–81, https://doi.org/10.3138/ijfab-2023-0008

almost grieving the loss of coping mechanisms that have served me most of my life. Most days see the return of muscle twitches, of the sinking feeling but not in a catastrophic way, a little bit of wanting to curl up and hide.

But there's a kitchen renovation to organise and post-surgery eye drops four times a day and trying out driving, doing errands, being with an offspring who's come to stay a few weeks.

Andrew comments that — whether good or bad — I've talked far more about my mother in this last year than ever before. I've obviously been in denial most of my life.

I read an emailed response to questions I'd asked regarding the result of my complaint to the Psychotherapists' Board.

'I haven't enough eyeball left to roll any more,' I tell my family. The Board intermediary hasn't answered my key questions and backtracked on others, too obviously and nervously trying to cover their tail. It's such a mess. I'm angry and upset, and then when Andrew comes home, he's full of his day. I realise there's no point talking to him in detail as he doesn't like complaints — it's just not him... and there it goes, I'm in shutdown mode again. Don't want to, can't, talk or interact with anyone without a supreme effort, and when I do, it's like watching a movie rather than being there.

I take off to a beach by myself after tea, desperate for space. It's a beautiful early summer evening. Two young girls play cricket with driftwood wickets, various sizes of dogs enjoy the sights and smells, a driftwood wigwam structure testifies to someone's earlier creativity. I stay till the sun dips behind the hill circling the bay and go home, very reluctantly.

I don't want to be part of this hurtful world. It's not quite suicidal ideation, but very close. Well, maybe it is. I did think about what it would be like walking into the water — with no intent, just wondering. Take your shoes off? Would survival just kick in? How far out would you have to swim, and at a beach like this? The odds are someone would notice and come to the rescue.

My muscles are tense and the next day I'm exhausted; my eye hurts; I take paracetamol, get breakfast in bed, and go back to sleep.

It takes days to recover.

I talk to my sister. She says that we never went to our mother when we were hurt as kids: we always went to our dad. She thinks our mother had postpartum depression after having me.

'I remember when you were little one time that Dad was in the hallway with Mum. He was holding onto both of Mum's upper arms, trying to calm down her hysteria.'

So, my pre-verbal years were formed with a mother who had back pain, a major spinal operation (my sisters can't remember who looked after me while our mother was in hospital), probable untreated postnatal depression, and a total inability to accept responsibility for looking after children who were hurt or sick. Or in other words, who were less than perfect. She wouldn't accept anyone else as human, and she wouldn't accept any responsibility in her actions or lack of action towards us. It was always, always, someone else's fault.

I mention to my sister my nightmares after our mother died.

'Why did you bring Mum down to Wellington to go into a rest home?'

I say it was to protect Tina from the daily phone call of emotional dumping, and who else was around who could do it?

'I always wondered. I was in awe of you. I couldn't have done it, myself,' says June.

I'm speechless.

. . .

The Christmas break begins.

'We're on holiday!' Andrew happily comments.

'*You're* on holiday', I reply.

He looks sidelong at me and repeats, 'We're on holiday.'

'No,' I say quietly. 'What am I "on holiday" from?'

I describe this interchange in therapy.

'It sounds like there's a lot of anger there,' she comments. 'Anger is good — it has energy. We can work with anger more easily than depression.'

I immediately feel a panicky response, shift tack in the conversation; I'm tearing up and I feel a long way off being okay to cry in therapy. We discuss suicidal thoughts again, but I can't bring myself to describe the last fleeting thought about that this morning. She clarifies that any therapist must sign off that they *will* give clients the community mental health team details, because that's 'ethical', and her not doing so for me could be cause for complaint against her.

'Not from my family,' I state emphatically.

She thinks the community mental health set-up may help perhaps 'one in ten'. Not exactly a great hit rate. What if other parts of the health system only helped ten per cent of their patients?

'How we are doing in our therapeutic relationship — how's it going here?', she asks suddenly, gesturing to me and herself.

I feel panicky again. Since when has anyone ever checked in to see how a relationship is for me?

I tear up writing this in my diary entry for the day.

With one of our offspring home on a visit, I share a few more childhood memories. As usual her jaw drops. I share about my mother's comment on how relaxing breastfeeding was, when my eldest was a toddler and the next sibling just a baby, when any normal grandmother would see it was NOT relaxing for me with my other responsibilities and would be reading to or interacting with the toddler. And that look on my mother's face, a look of self-focused, oblivious joy — why did it make me feel so ick, so disgusted? Was that what I was to her as a baby — just something to relax her?

My youngest shares memories of me asking her every day after school how her day was. I reflect that I have no memory of this in my childhood. It may have happened. But I don't recall. I remember coming home sometimes to delicious fresh pikelets which I could load butter on to, or homemade chocolate square. But I don't recall interaction with me, about me, about my day.

Christmas Day comes, and another Dungeons & Dragons session, a fight against an Ancient Green Dragon with Feeble Mind previously cast on it. A Schleich dragon from our children's childhood collection and a selection of my Lego minifigs set the scene. I reflect once more how much D&D values the individual skills of vastly different, very damaged characters banding together and coming up with the goods in very difficult situations. I'm super proud of our DM, our Dungeon Master. Empathy and leadership skills are great traits to have in a DM.

At Christmas dinner with the extended family, the prospect of someone's mother dying hovers over the conversation. Someone acknowledges their grief, and states half-jokingly they are going to be horrible to their kids so that they won't have to feel like this one day. I quietly argue that it's far better for them to grieve the loss of love received than to have the nightmares I had after my mother's death.

In the peace of the day after Christmas I have time alone. I fall to thinking about my younger self. For a moment, briefly, for the first time, I see the younger me — who is in my mind's eye, always head bowed, arms hanging over legs bent at the knees, sitting back against a wall — looking up and looking at me. We connect. I see in surprise the face of an older version of me than I expected. There's some kind of fusion, some recognition: this younger me, is me. The image is only there briefly. Then it vanishes.

TESTING, READY OR NOT

'Most mental health practitioners are not trained to identify complex trauma and dissociation in their clients.'

— Lynette S. Danylchuk and Kevin J. Connors, 'Treating Complex Trauma and Dissociation: A Practical Guide to Navigating Therapeutic Challenges', 2nd ed. (New York: Routledge, 2023)

Health assessment inevitably comes with questionnaires, whether openly acknowledged or hidden in the conversation with your health professional.

For the first EMDR therapist I try, there's a dissociation questionnaire for me to fill in beforehand.

It is the Dissociative Experiences Scale.

My score on that was so normal, even lower than normal, that I suspected a problem. I knew very little about dissociation at this point. But I was beginning to realise this was a key to understanding my problem.

My first reaction to any problem being more research, I looked around the website for the questionnaire the therapist had given me. I find one that assessed how 'shut down' you are: the Shut-D test — D for Dissociation.*

Where the average healthy person would score between 1 and 3 on this test, I get a 9.

This doesn't seem high, until I read down further in the interpretation of results section.

Nine is higher than major depressive disorder, psychotic spectrum disorder, schizophrenia. It's not high enough to match the average score for borderline personality disorder or dissociative identity disorder. But it is undeniably high.

A year later, on starting with my sixth therapist, I take the test again — not at her suggestion, but for myself, to give me a baseline. This time I score 6. That's still high.

Not long after beginning to delve into the world of trauma, I inevitably discover the ACE studies. ACE stands for Adverse Childhood Events: the original research questionnaire from the late 1990s lists ten highly stressful things that may have occurred in

---

* http://traumadissociation.com/shut-d

your childhood. A score of four or more different ACEs is so alarmingly linked to a higher likelihood of many terrible health outcomes that I wonder why I've never heard of it before. My score is 3, though on reflection for the first couple of decades of my adult life I would have self-assessed as only 1 or 2 — I had repressed my memory of sexual abuse. That is sobering. I think that 3 is not too bad, all things considered, until I see that it still puts my score in the top quarter of the (American) population. And I have issues with the questions: there's no measure of how long something went on for, no measure of how one small thing can loom large in the context of overall neglect, and it is oddly specific — I can't score for physical violence because it was not me or my mother who was hit, but my big sister, by my mother. It feels ill-suited for neglect — the events that didn't happen, the relationships that should have been there but weren't.

I discover the Childhood Trauma Questionnaire.* This one puts my childhood into much sharper focus. It covers physical abuse, emotional abuse, sexual abuse, physical neglect, and emotional neglect — all of which are covered in the ACE questionnaire. But here, each type of adversity is not just simply marked present or absent but ranked on a numerical scale for severity and then divided into levels — None, Low, Moderate, Severe. My scores show there was no physical abuse or physical neglect, no emotional abuse, only low levels of sexual abuse (that I can remember). But the score for emotional neglect is breathtaking: in the 20s. The highest possible score is 25. The level for Severe is anything above 18.

In May 2023, after finishing EMDR and waiting to get into the public health system, I take the online Depression, Anxiety, and

---

* https://www.researchgate.net/publication/336531235_CHILD_TRAUMA_QUESTIONAIRE_CTQ_SHORT_FORM_-_A_RE-DESIGN_OF_CTQ-SF

Stress test.* The website now says you should only take the test with a health practitioner.

My scores are 29, 6, 14.

29 means 'Extremely Severe' depression

6 is just below 7, the 'Normal' level of anxiety

14 means 'Extremely Severe' levels of stress.

'You should seek the advice of a medical professional immediately', the website notes on my results.

Ah, if only it were that simple.

In the early months of my collapse, listening to podcast after podcast on trauma, I feel so puzzled. The first EMDR therapist, like many of these podcasts and books on trauma, insisted that every trauma survivor has the symptom of low self-worth, along with a harsh 'inner critic'.

I can't relate. I don't have the classic signs of this. I check with one of my offspring: she likewise sees no such negative self-reference in me. I trust my kids' judgements far more than anyone who has only met me for less than an hour.

The next EMDR provider is fine with this 'core belief'. She says that everyone is different. Some do have a core belief, an unconscious, foundational framework for the world, that they are worthless: but not all. The best trauma experts talk of how varied the experience is of traumatised people, how individual each treatment plan must be. Dr Ham, the New York psychologist who treated Stephanie Foo, talks of being asked to write a book on how he 'does' his therapy: he replies that he would rather publish a book with 300 blank pages, and give it to his clients, so that they may tell their story.† Despite many clinicians and practitioners building a

---

* https://www.depression-anxiety-stress-test.org

† Dr Jacob Ham: 'What Really Helps Trauma?', YouTube, 21 November 2023, @Forrest Hanson

career on the foundation of the one successful treatment mode they have developed, no one mode will help every survivor. There is no magic formula. There are now a lot more options for treatment. If you can find and afford them.

After a while I decide to find some online quizzes about self-esteem.

Psychology Today's test* comes in at 81/100, Moderately High — the second highest level. As I suspected, if anything, my self-esteem is a little too high.

I try the Rosenberg Self Esteem test:† 23/30. Anything below 15 is considered low self-esteem.

I love the comments from this website.

> *This test will probably not tell you anything you do not already know. You should have a pretty good grasp of your results just by asking yourself the question, 'do I have low self-esteem?' The scale can however give you a better picture of your state in relation to other people.*

I try a different tack, a self-compassion test.‡ This is a bit more nuanced, with five sub-themes. I score a bit on the high side for Isolation and Over-Identification, but my overall score is 3.16. On the scale of 1 to 5, the test results state that the average is around 3. My self-compassion, overall, is quite average.

Even in the world of those with trauma, I'm a bit of an oddity. I reach out in an online support group — does anyone else here relate? A few reply, yes. They don't have low self-esteem. They are all either neurodiverse as well as traumatised or have suffered an unspeakably horrible childhood. I read up the acronym one of them mentions: RAD. Reactive Attachment Disorder. The diagnostic

---

* https://www.psychologytoday.com/nz/tests/personality/self-esteem-test
† https://openpsychometrics.org/tests/RSE.php
‡ https://self-compassion.org/self-compassion-test/

criteria make for chilling reading. The kind of childhood, the level of abuse and lack of care required to result in such a disorder, is horrific.*

---

* https://traumadissociation.com/rad

INTENSITY

'Trauma recovery can be hard for survivors of neglect, because it asks us to pay attention to our feelings & acknowledge them as important. We don't have a lot of experience w/that. It feels weird. "Wrong". Like a trick.
We're not used to our feelings, or our needs, mattering.'

— Dr Glenn Doyle: Instagram, 9 December 2023, @DrDoyleSays

'This is the most intense session you've had yet,' my therapist sums up at the end of our thirteenth session.

I kind of knew where this one was going — at some point, attachment and my inner child would turn up as things to experience or process.

The session started as usual. I make a comment on the weather, she responds, a pause, then the gentle: 'So, how are you going?'

I'm momentarily at a loss. I just never know how to answer the 'how are you?' question, even with a person I'm literally paying to ask such questions.

'I had a funny incident on the way here... I went to the chemist to pick up something, and remembering we were almost out of paracetamol, I asked the assistant if it was possible to buy two 100-packs. "I'll let you buy two packs of paracetamol if you promise not to take them all at once," she'd said in a half-joking awkward way. I looked her straight in the eye and said, "I can promise you I wouldn't do it with these." She didn't really respond and just sold me both packs.'

My therapist's face shows the slight sense of horror I can't let myself feel.

'What did that bring up for you?'

Well, memories of very unpleasant times last year, I guess.

Warmed up, I'm able to tell her about the catastrophising I've done this week, the thoughts that something awful is going to happen to one of my kids, the thoughts that I'm going to have a heart attack here in therapy, and what would she do then as she doesn't even have any emergency contact details?

'A heart attack! How interesting. What do you think that means? Are you worried you won't survive if you show what you feel, here? How long did it go on for?'

'It stops as soon as I name it as catastrophising,' I reply.

'Wow. Could you bottle that? It would be helpful! How would I know you are dissociating here? What might that look like?'

We talk about that a little. I'm reminded of my panic attack before my second EMDR session.

'Just checking in, are we doing okay, here in this relationship?'

I reply honestly for once — 'It's a work in progress' — with a wry smile.

And all at once I feel like I'm starting to float away on a cloud. I say that out loud.

'Yes, I feel your floating feeling too. Right. Put your feet on the ground, let's stay here…'

'I forgot to bring the tennis ball I talked about last time,' I flounder. I need something to hold onto.

I'm offered a very brightly coloured soft but spiky ball. I try it but it's not quite right. I put it aside.

'Here, try a cushion, to put a barrier between you and me, to help you feel safe, if you want.'

So, there I am, at fifty-five, on a firm couch in a large lounge room with a beautiful view and all I can do is tear up and hug the cushion and look steadfastly at the floor and manage to say it feels odd to be so like a child.

'Yes, and I'm not saying this to be demeaning, but the little girl Robyn is here. She's been here every session, checking me out, and that's okay. It's up to her when she wants to show up and when she doesn't. It's okay to feel like that. I've had middle-aged people on that couch looking like a baby. It's very strong, it's very natural.'

She reassures me that I'm the expert on me, that I'm in control here, that I don't have to talk about or 'do' anything here that I don't want to: that I'm a brave wahine*. I talk about memories of a lost teddy bear, and she says how important those toys are, like I'd know with my kids, and yes, did I ever know that from parenting our kids. She reflects on my catastrophising, suggesting the 'heart attack' I've feared may be the overload of emotion, the broken heart of my small child self, that I don't want to feel.

---

* 'wahine' is the Māori word for 'woman'

For the first time a therapist has suggested a link I hadn't already made myself or dismissed as incorrect, and I'm in awe of her skill and compassion. She suggests she could be given some emergency contact details — to help me feel safe, not because she needs it, nor in any kind of form-filling, this-must-be-done way. I realise then, I've not filled out a single form for her, not been given any written info other than her website, no paperwork of any kind. I realise how different this is from other health professionals who prefer to hide behind forms and crisis phone numbers and cover-themselves-ness, without taking the time to see what impact that has on the client. It's incredibly refreshing.

I calm down, slowly, talking about another memory — running for a plane down a long hallway in a Mexican or American airport, age five, my short legs not keeping up with the rest of the family. In my memory everyone is so much taller than me, running away, not looking back, not waiting for me, not acknowledging my inability to keep up: I feel the stress, and I feel like I'm being left behind.

At the end I get up from the couch with an automatic 'thank you', and she looks at me pointedly.

'You don't have to say thank you.'

She goes on with other words to show she knows what that session took out of me, how hard it is, and that being polite about it is probably an ingrained, inauthentic response. I give a small, tired smile and say I'll remember that. I have tears coming to my eyes on and off all the way home.

My household are very sweet and understanding.

I wake at midnight, tense. Bathroom, paracetamol, and sleepily try to see if little Robyn wants to be introduced to the lovely grown-ups who she can trust and rely on — the therapist, my husband, a couple of close friends. My own grown-up self, even.

HEALING IS NOT LINEAR

'The journey to healing from complex trauma is not for the faint of heart. I don't know a more difficult journey that one can take, than to heal from complex trauma. ...
It is not a death sentence. It takes a ton of work, but there is a way out.'

— Tim Fletcher: YouTube, 'New Thoughts About Complex Trauma Part 1/4', 21 April 2019, @Tim Fletcher

HEALING IS NOT LINEAR

Four months into psychotherapy, I abruptly text my therapist.

'I need a break from therapy. Please don't hold my spot.'

I'm exhausted from yesterday's session, from the bad night's sleep that follows, from the unspeakably painful trauma response. I've had it.

Therapy has been a struggle. I still can't seem to bring myself to feel safe enough to experience any strong emotion in her presence, but those feelings are sitting there like an undersea volcano about to erupt. It has been a dance, so far: for many sessions I report on how I reacted badly to something she said or did in the last one, things I can't report on as it happens, because I'm so shut off from my feelings. She mostly apologises, talking about the time it takes to get to know each other. After a couple of months, she pushes back a little, saying she is a different human being from me. We are two different minds. She is going, inevitably, to say or do something that I don't like. She cannot always work around my every wish, not without losing her own authentic self. She says she is furious with how I've been treated by health professionals, by the system: but that alone will not help me.

I don't like it. My infant-level emotions want perfect mirroring, perfect attunement, perfect focus. All the basic building blocks of being a human being that I didn't, clearly, get. I push back especially hard anytime I hear advice. Advice is not what I came for, I say.

Our sixteenth session feels like it backfires badly.

I'd had a distressing phone call from a family member. I'd had a response to following up on my complaint about the last therapist, that had taken five months and some chasing up to receive at all, that even my ever-positive husband described as 'perfunctory'.

The therapist leans forward.

'Robyn, I strongly suggest you not take the complaint any further. What do you want from the process?'

'Justice, I guess… to be seen, to have recognition of the harm I felt.'

'You won't get it. The system isn't set up for that. Putting your energy into learning how to deal with the feelings that keep arising in these kinds of situations, that go on repeat all through your life — that's what needs to happen. You're angry, rightly so. Can you sit with that feeling…?'

Very quickly the answer is clear. I can't.

My head begins to lower, bowed, broken, trying to block out the other human sitting just opposite and the pain inside. Eye contact stops.

'What are you feeling?'

I can't respond beyond a slight shake of the head, mutely staring at a patch of carpet just beyond my feet.

She leans forward slightly, focused, trying to see my face, trying to tell me how therapy would be good for me if I participated rather than use avoidance tactics, trying to sell me the benefits of what life could be like for me. It feels like a generic pep talk. I can barely respond.

She tries to bring me back to the present, but I'm gone.

'We've got five more minutes. Is there anything else you want to say?'

With more hesitation than I expected to feel, I manage to stumble out that I'm deeply uneasy at her verbalising over the last two sessions that she does care about me.

She looks intently in another direction, as she often does when reflecting on her actions.

'I'm sorry. That was too early. Maybe you will manage to hear that in another six months.'

Six months? The words clang in my brain. I'm that broken. Six months!

The reaction in the early hours of the next morning is vicious.

At 2 am I wake up and start planning how I could get my hands on suicide means. I'd gone back to sleep fairly quickly, but in the morning, I awake exhausted, shut down, wandering in and out of actively suicidal thoughts. The thought of doing more therapy seems impossible. This intense pain, the desperation to get rid of it, to never feel this bad again: this is the reason I persisted so long in finding therapy, only now to find that even therapy triggers unbearable pain. I can't take it.

Her response to my text helps begin thawing my anger and frozen pain.

Whatever had happened to cause distress in the session, whatever she'd said, she really wants the opportunity to repair it with me. She asks me to reconsider meeting again.

I feel sufficiently bad at causing upset in her that I send an explanatory email.

And then the next day, I swallow my pride and shame and hurt.

I text. 'Is it okay to change my mind and come next week...? At least to discuss how I can better manage being in therapy?'

It takes three days to start feeling better.

The next therapy session is one of the most awkward interactions I have ever experienced. I am still angry. Why didn't she see I was so distressed last time? Why did she keep talking at me? I read out my written response, unable to just say it, feeling a growing sense of shame as I do so. Why do I keep overreacting to what she's saying and doing? Why am I so everlastingly angry?

Somehow, we manage to talk it through. She looks unusually serious, without her warm smile, and looks somewhat bemused.

'Your dissociation isn't very obvious, Robyn!... What would you want me to do, when it happens again?'

'Just tell me you think I may be dissociating, or in distress... Just ask me about that. Don't lecture me, don't just keep on going.'

We reach an agreement that if I ever want to pause or stop therapy again like this, when something has 'gone wrong', I will come back for one more session. She says how much she appreciates my coming back this time, she sees how hard that is to do. She doesn't assume I'll be back next week, giving me permission to have the break I thought I needed, talking through options if I do come back to go more slowly, to 'pause' by just having sessions talking about trauma at an intellectual level rather than try to work through it.

But now I realise, I need to come back. I can't go on being a walking volcano.

No-one else I've reached out to for help has a good enough idea of how to help.

Most have simply made things much, much worse.

There's nowhere left to go.

As we head to the door at the session end, I make some comment about my text or email, and her face looks stricken.

'I was devastated,' she says, simply, honestly, with deep feeling.

Somehow these words sneak in among the thick walls of my feeling fortress. This person cares deeply, but is also professional, experienced. She's been here before with clients. She's stared death in the face with us, so many times. She's not afraid of anything I may say or do, it seems, except a client walking out on therapy with no attempt at resolution.

This is one of many sessions where she uses the word 'repair'.

'You've had so much rupture and no repair. It's not me being perfectly attuned to you that will help you: it's us working together to make the repair after a rupture.'

In the following months we talk about the book I'm writing. She encourages me to bring some in, if I like.

The first time I bring my writing, I'm a bit unsure. Do I want to read this, or get her to read it?

'How about you try?' she says.

'I'm not here to appraise what you've done as a piece of writing, as a publisher or critic would: whether the writing is "good" or not is beside the point.'

I look down at the printed pages.

'Go slowly, don't make it an intellectual exercise Robyn, try to be with the feelings that arise.'

I nod, hardly hearing. I really just want an audience for my writing. Maybe this could be another way to avoid feeling anything in session, though this thought is barely conscious. I have no expectation that anything beyond some praise will happen.

I start to read.

And I choke up. Like a portal to another world, memories I have so clinically typed up at home now begin to come to life inside me, in the presence of this professional, compassionate witness.

This first passage I read aloud is about my two worst waking nightmares. I glance up only occasionally. I pause now and then, an unfamiliar sense of feeling uncomfortable, painful emotions without starting to shut down, without feeling like it is all out of control.

I also feel a bubbling up inside, like a lid off a bottle of fizzy drink, an odd childlike sense of excited achievement. We've found a way in. I can begin to learn how to feel my own emotions, when someone else is around, without having to be on guard as to what she might feel or what her reaction may be, with all the decades of defences peeling away.

There is no dramatic sobbing. This is not the movies; it is not *Good Will Hunting*. My pauses are still short, tentative. But we've started.

DARKNESS VISIBLE

Alongside my two worst waking nightmares are two nightmare visions.
I don't remember if they came to me in my dreams, or in waking hours.

I know them from early childhood, somewhere between five and ten years old, at a guess. But they returned to me at times then, and occasionally later. They haunt my early memories, ghostly shadows. They contain a world of pain and suffering I could find no way to understand or process, as a child.

One is a vision, a still image, of my mother's bare back. There is talcum powder on it, something she used after showering. I don't know if anyone uses it much now or whether it was even old-fashioned then; but it floated everywhere in the family's one bathroom. And though there are no visible marks or scars I see on her back — despite her spinal operation, when I was a toddler — I see somehow broken glass, not real but as if it is showing on the outside the brokenness of her body within. I feel that her back is causing much pain. And I don't know what to do with that pain.

The other vision, another still image, still more haunting.

From the age of six when we moved back to New Zealand, I had my own bedroom, small, but mine alone. Its wide, sole window faced the street that could not be seen, because our house was down a steep bank, our roof barely level with the roadway. It was a new build, two two-bedroom townhouses joined together, built on the site of a former butcher shop. There was no landscaping done, just the steep driveway. My dad started digging out front to begin a garden. He discovered old concrete steps from the street level where the shop had once stood; he kept digging down and found the concrete floor of the old butcher shop basement. He found metal meat hooks. He made a retaining wall, moved soil in metal buckets to an unusable but accessible area under our house, under my bedroom; made crazy paving paths from the concrete pad to the back door. A garden was planted.

In my vision, I look out my window and see my sister, hung from a rope, above the concrete floor that now forms our garden patio.

It makes no sense. There is no tree there, nothing to hang a rope from, but I know the body is there, hanging, perhaps twitching; the image is unclear, and I don't see her face, I just know it is her. It is terrifying.

Now, decades later, I wonder about the source of such an image. To the best of my knowledge, hanging is not one of the methods my sister Tina attempted. She tried several ways while I was at primary school. Not hanging. I do not recall this method being described by my mother — and she did describe several, actual and potential, in my hearing, as a young child.

There was no internet until I was an adult. I watched limited television — mostly what our mother watched in the evening: British comedies, dramas. I don't recall anything that could be linked to that nightmare vision. I don't recall reading any novels with such scenes until I was at least fifteen, reading Thomas Hardy's *Tess of the D'Urbervilles*, and by this time my sister no longer lived at home. Perhaps my sense of time is off, perhaps I didn't have this vision as early as I think I do. It floats, solid but untethered, a nightmare not dreamt, a sight not seen but somehow felt.

A week after my election loss in 2022, the first suicidal image that pops into my mind is of me hanging by a rope, in the place I am sitting. This time there is somewhere a rope could be hung from, but I recoil from this horrific, intrusive thought. I would never want to hang myself. End this pain, yes, end my life somehow, but not that way.

The image is brief, but it takes a few weeks to re-enter that place without a slight shudder.

Eighteen months later, feeling a bit better after months of therapy, I stumbled across a record on our National Archives website. It's for a great-aunt who died when I was ten, and whom I'm sure I never met. Madge. The record is dated simply 1914–5. It's from Seaview, a mental hospital.

I don't recall our mother ever referring to this episode in her aunt's life. It happened years before my mother was born, and most likely she was never told. I knew my great-aunt was the musical one, the piano teacher, and that's about all.

A couple of days after requesting the document, it arrives.

It's a few brief but revealing pages of patient notes.

And in it, this line: 'Her little brother found her one day with a rope round her neck.'

My great-aunt, also, knew what it was like to want to die.

It's rather... unsettling.

I'm reassured by the relative briefness of her stay, the care shown in the notes, her mother's honesty (did her husband ever know he was noted in medical records as being bad-tempered?), and the holistic range of questions asked of the patient and her family. The treatment was complete bed rest, milk diet with raw eggs, and a sedative when needed. No lobotomies here. I'm grateful.

She had three younger brothers. In 1915 they were sixteen, fourteen, and eight.

Was it the eight-year-old who found his oldest sister with a rope around her neck?

Please God, no. Would the mother have described him as 'her little brother', or 'her littlest brother'? I'm clutching at straws.

My grandmother — the next oldest living daughter — was nineteen. What did she see?

Was that haunting memory passed down, somehow, two generations below?

Or was it just a general cultural knowledge surfacing, perhaps there'd been a reading about the death of Judas in church I'd heard as a little girl, perhaps unconsciously I've always 'known' that killing yourself is by default, with a rope?

Unknown. Unsettling.

Unsettling to see that psychiatric care has regressed, at least in this case, since 1915.

Unsettling how random is the sufficiency of care for those who are in such acute distress.

FLUFFY GREEK HERO

'Here's the deal. The human soul doesn't want to be advised or fixed or saved.
It simply wants to be witnessed — to be seen, heard and companioned exactly as it is.'

— Parker J. Palmer: 'The Gift of Presence, The Perils of Advice', 27 April 2016, onbeing.org/blog

In April, six months into psychotherapy, I miss a week as we take a road trip south to see our daughter for her birthday.

This time, unlike the previous year, we trim back our expectations. It's a shorter break, less driving, fewer people to see. Another offspring has moved to Christchurch for postgraduate study. The family plan a sightseeing trip or two. On the second day they decide to go to the Antarctic Centre. I sense I need time alone, so I stay at the apartment we've rented. I want to write, and I manage a couple of thousand words for the morning. I feel better for it.

The family come back excited. They've bought a small stuffed toy, a husky that growls when you press it, for the birthday sibling. They talk about seeing the real huskies. Everyone talks about seeing another, bigger toy husky in the gift shop, one they really think I'd like. We make plans to go back there the next day.

The moment I see the dog on the shelf, I knew what my family were talking about. Somehow this one is for me. He's big enough to hug, with eyes and facial expression that holds my attention, giving me 'I'm there for you' feelings. His fake fur is white with a grey back and grey between his eyes: his ears and snout are endearingly not totally symmetrical: he wears a brown suede chest harness. He's a working dog.

There's a lot of talk about his name. There are suggestions, but I'm adamant.

This one is Ajax. I need his strength. I need the reminder that going it alone is not a good idea, no matter how strong you feel. I need the reminder that unresolved shame can be deadly.

Over the months to come, Ajax comes with me to therapy, to new places, to the doctor. My husband starts to put him beside me in bed when he gets up in the morning. Many mornings, he comes back with the customary cup of tea, to find Ajax getting a big hug. Ajax reminds me somehow, when I can't remember properly, just how much my own family loves me. I post photos on social media of him and me and often our cat too, stretched out on our sunny window seat. I love the way people respond to seeing him. Reading their responses or watching their faces light up when they see him in person… is healing, somehow. And funny. He's realistic enough to make people look twice.

One week I deliberately leave Ajax behind, not wanting the therapist to see him that week.

She notices the moment she opens the door.

'No Ajax this week?'

I confess in the following weeks that I left Ajax behind as some kind of punishment for her, an expression of my anger. It seems silly and futile and childish, but she takes it seriously and understands. Some weeks for a while afterwards she deliberately says 'Goodbye, Ajax' as we take our leave.

One week I mention I plan to take Ajax with me to my second university lecture.

The therapist looks concerned. She's worried I might get some negativity, but I have already sounded out my lecturer, asked to introduce Ajax as my support dog. He'd commented that the next lecture is going to be full of doom and gloom, so introducing something positive at the end would be great.

The lecture was indeed a gloomy summary of political realities in the world of policymaking. I turn around from my seat at the front of the class, hold Ajax aloft, and explain: 'This is Ajax, my support dog for complex trauma. He's not real — I can't have a real one — so he's very happy if you want to come by anytime for a pat. He won't bite!'

Afterwards one woman exclaims to me, 'I could have done with that last lecture! I need to pet a dog.'

Another man, about a decade younger than me, approaches with a lovely grin. He focuses on Ajax, and gives him a pat.

'I have kids, my son has a soft toy animal like this.' It's said with beautiful, simple understanding and not a whiff of condescension, but rather pure delight in something that reminds him of his beloved child.

On the commute home, an alert grey-haired woman enters the crowded railway station toilet where I'm the last in the queue, by the door. The main women's toilets are out of order and there are worried faces all round. Ajax is stuffed into a red and blue backpack for our public transport trips, head poking out, resting on the floor beside me while I wait. The woman sees him, is taken aback, looks up at me quickly and back down to Ajax, bursting into a huge, surprised, motherly smile.

And then it strikes me, what Ajax means to me.

He embodies the way I want people to respond to me, or more particularly, the way I needed my parents to respond — with open-faced, obvious delight, with focused attention, with care and compassion.

Ajax is also the happy child face of me that I had to put on as a mask, rather than let my parents see my real emotions. Because they couldn't handle real emotions. Not their own, not their children's.

I explain that in therapy.

'It's like he gives me some space, some distance: Ajax gets the positive attention, and I get it through him.'

The therapist pauses in thought.

'What would it feel like to experience that attention directly, yourself?' she asks.

'Dangerous,' I reply.

I buy Ajax a personalised dog tag that reads *Trauma Support Dog* with a symbol I assume to be the traditional medical one, and on the reverse, his name and my phone number, in case he gets lost.

I look more closely at the symbol. It's a staff with wings at its top, entwined by two serpents. According to Wikipedia it's called the caduceus, and it is different from the usual medical symbol, the

Rod of Asclepius, which bears no wings and only one snake. The caduceus is the rod of Hermes, Greek messenger to the gods.

I'm glad it's not the medical symbol. The world of medicine has done as much harm as good to me, if not more.

Ajax sits with me as I wrestle with writing, as I try to be a messenger for whatever gods there may be.

WASTING TIME

'Over the years our research team has repeatedly found that chronic emotional abuse and neglect can be just as devastating as physical abuse and sexual molestation.'

— Dr Bessel van der Kolk, 'The Body Keeps the Score'

In my late forties the second of our two cats died, both much younger than expected. We thought we'd get a puppy instead this time. It would be great to get us walking more, it would be good company for me. We were down to two offspring living at home. The empty nest was looming, perhaps.

We'd looked after someone's fully grown dog while they were on holiday. I did loads of research on puppy training. I found a gorgeous-looking breed of dog known to be very social. The whole family was very excited.

The reality was quite different.

I didn't realise how used I was to having cats, who spend a lot of their day independently and, with a cat flap, can be quickly trained to go outside when needed. This puppy was so very different. Within ten days I was at a breakdown. I was told she couldn't be left outside until much older, in case someone stole her to use for dogfighting or resale. The responsibility for its training fell largely on me, given I was home all day, but this just made me feel trapped. We couldn't work out how to stop the puppy using her teeth on our bare legs in the mornings or on hot days. I felt like a failure. We rang the dog breeder who sized up the situation very quickly and found a new home for her.

I was shaken to the core. This was just a puppy. How could a puppy get to me this way? Why was I so stressed out? Why couldn't I grit my teeth and get through the first few difficult months, knowing this puppy phase doesn't last? What happens if something else like this, some other thing I can't anticipate, happens in future, that I can't get rid of or ask to be taken back?

A friend recommended a counsellor. I got in touch, made an appointment. I knew nothing of the world of counselling or therapy or who I should talk to. Instinctively I felt that something from my past must be causing problems. I just knew I was badly in need of help.

At the appointment, the man sitting across from me was maybe a little younger than me. I quickly outlined what my problem was and my fears about something happening again in future, if I didn't sort myself out.

The reaction was not what I expected.

Within a very short time I felt totally humiliated. The counsellor could barely conceal his incredulity that a puppy would cause such a response in me. 'I have a dog,' he said, looking at me with puzzled eyes. His message was clear: my response wasn't normal. I think he therefore concluded that it wasn't that much of a problem, that I was overstating it for attention; when he found out I was *just* a stay-at-home mother, he made his conclusion obvious. I was wasting his time, an overprivileged white woman with nothing better to do, no 'real' problem to explore. When I tried to ask whether something in my past could do this, he batted that away with an 'explanation' of the latest psychology, that 'we don't go digging around in the past anymore, that's not helpful'.

What about my future? I thought.

I did not know then what I do now. My response to the puppy was an overreaction, an abnormally big reaction. That is a hallmark of trauma. It's called emotional dysregulation.

My perception that I couldn't escape a responsibility that felt overwhelming triggered a response from deep in my past.

I walked away from that appointment and put it behind me. Getting help was obviously useless. It had just made me feel ashamed of my reaction, which I now tried my best to forget. We could of course avoid getting a puppy in future. What we couldn't avoid was anything else that would trigger a breakdown. We didn't even know what those triggers might be, and I had no tools or support to understand just how critically important this was. I used the tried-and-true tactic: denial.

OF TEDDY BEARS AND GUINEA PIGS

'A key aspect of What happened to you? is What didn't happen for you? — what attention, nurturing touch, reassurance — basically, what love — didn't you get?
I realised that neglect is as toxic as trauma.'

— Bruce Perry: 'What Happened to You? Conversations on Trauma, Resilience, and Healing'

The next story I should tell is about the replacement teddy and the dead guinea pigs.

I feel reluctant. It feels quite trivial, the replacement teddy. Someone will think I was just a spoiled ungrateful brat. Like many of my memories, it feels very much like a 'first-world problem'.

What do I have to complain about?

And yet... I tell this story to my therapist, and she nods, understanding.

On my first or second birthday, there's a photo of me with my three big sisters, on a small concrete landing outside our North Shore suburban home in Auckland. I'm sitting on a ride-on toy, holding a picture book and a blue-and-white teddy bear about half the size of me. I don't look that happy. My sisters, or at least one of them, smiles for the camera as you are supposed to.

That teddy goes with me for our six months' stay in Wellington and then to Jamaica.

I don't have a memory of that teddy. I do remember casually mentioning the teddy bear, a few years after coming back, maybe aged nine or ten. I must have mentioned to someone in the family that I'd missed him. He was lost, never making it back home to New Zealand with us.

A few days later I entered my bedroom, and with shock saw a small teddy bear sitting up against my bed pillow. He's deep orange and white, and small, and ugly, and... who bought this for me? Why? I'm confused. How am I meant to respond? I don't want another teddy bear: I feel embarrassed, too old for a soft toy. Unconsciously I know, what bear could possibly replace the companion of my preschool years? It must have been one of my parents, but which one? How am I supposed to react to a gift I don't want?

No-one says anything. I feel awkward. I made some comments about the nice teddy bear. I give it a name.

I didn't know then, but I didn't need my loss 'fixed'. I needed my feelings of loss seen and heard and understood. I didn't need something bought for me; I needed something witnessed in me. I needed to be seen. Whoever bought the teddy bear did not want their child to feel the pain of loss. I get that. But that's the job of a parent, to sit with their child in uncomfortable feelings, to develop in them the tools to cope with loss and pain and anger and all the messiness of human life.

Things don't fix feelings.

I talk with one of my sisters. Not about the bear, about other things.

'Mum must have changed after I left home. I don't remember her being like you say. I remember this time when we had guinea pigs, before you were born, and they died. We were so sad. Mum took us out to buy new gumboots or raincoats or something. We didn't have much money then, so it was a big deal to get something new.'

My sister didn't say anything about being hugged, being listened to, being told it was okay to feel sad when a pet dies. She didn't talk about her mother helping with a burial. My sister felt consoled, because something was bought for her.

I really don't see a difference. Our mother couldn't bear the messiness of our emotions.

Buying things is the easy way out.

NOT THIS DAY AGAIN

Even when my own children were little, I disliked Mother's Day.

My kids didn't need a special day where they were told in Sunday School to make a card for me — they made them throughout the year, as they felt like it, to tell me how special I was to them.

I certainly didn't want to be reminded that I was a mother making huge and noble sacrifices for her children. What I wanted was the odd day off. I did go away for a weekend a year, for a few years, out of town and far away. It helped. Much as I love my kids, it's bloody hard work raising them without family support, with no break from the endless overwhelming responsibility of being the primary caregiver for a tiny vulnerable precious human being.

In the months after my election loss, I came face to face with the true impact of my childhood neglect, with how much I hate my mother. That's when Mother's Day took on new horrors.

Suddenly I notice there is a deluge of marketing emails with their propaganda around making mothers happy with 'thoughtful' gifts or meals. Anything and everything — pizza sides, plant nurseries. A new trend seems to be just starting where some companies let you opt out of their emails — only for this year — acknowledging that the day can be 'hard' for some. The implications usually are that it's hard because you've lost your mother recently, and the grief involved from a loss of her love is tough. I have yet to see a commercial company brave enough to acknowledge that the day might be tough for some, quite simply, because their mother was traumatic to be around.

In the first year after my election loss, I chose not to attend church that Mother's Day. I remembered the previous year it had been handled with great sensitivity, prayers and acknowledgements given up front as to the many reasons why the day would not be happy for some. But I felt that if someone was to inadvertently wish me 'Happy Mother's Day!' I'd be triggered, and not up to handling that.

This is the second year post loss. I haven't been to a church service in months. I feel like I could go. I'm feeling 'better'. I want to see a few people there who I don't see during the week otherwise; I feel able to cope with not taking part, simply being a spectator.

As for Mother's Day, I feel I can just say 'I don't celebrate it' should someone unknowingly say those meaningless, affronting words, words that allow no acknowledgement of the hell of my childhood, no acknowledgement of the gaping void left when a mother isn't up to her job. I feel sure the service would be sensitively handled as I recall before, and I feel up to risking it. My husband is pleasantly surprised but a little nervous.

'There will be Mother's Day stuff?' he says in the car.

'I do know what day it is,' I reply.

Not a single reference to Mother's Day that morning acknowledges the pain that its reminder can bring. I'm sitting beside someone who receives a happy Mother's Day greeting. When I comment firmly that I don't celebrate it, there is an insistence that I could still celebrate being a good mother myself.

I repeat, 'I don't celebrate Mother's Day. End of story.' I pause. I'm trying to find a reason the hearer will find acceptable to deal with and find something that half works.

'It's just a commercial invention to sell more stuff anyway.'

'Oh yes, it's about being together, not buying things,' comes the reply.

This logic clangs in my brain. It may be for you, I think, but for me, I've already said I don't celebrate it. Twice. Why be so insistent that I should? Does it spoil your day, knowing I don't? Make you uncomfortable? Why do you think I might feel like a bad mother, just because mine was? Why do I need the excuse of a certain day to be together with my family?

There is in the intercessory prayer a short, sanitised mention of mothers, thanking them for their huge sacrifices at their essential job. Clang. Sentimentalised nonsense. Nothing, again, about the pain some carry this day.

I walk out to the bathroom for a breather and return in time to hear the priest's invocation to give each other a sign of peace, 'and if the person looks like a mother, wish them a happy Mother's Day'.

I walk back out, take another breather. I don't think I'm triggered. I'm just sad, disappointed, let down, and angry. My church has done so, so much better than this in the recent past. The last thing I want today is more Mother's Day greetings.

I move back to my seat to retrieve my coat, to leave early. Someone innocently walks towards me, hand outstretched and smiling, wanting to wish me peace. I duck and shake my head, apologising, grab my coat, and walk out the door. Out on the street in the brighter light of day, I take a deep breath. I text my husband that I'm walking home, and off I walk. I feel a bit teary, a bit angry: a bit lost, because most of my adult life has centred around being part of a church, and even the little I'm getting out of it and giving to it now seems gone.

I wonder if it's time to face the fact that my part in a church may have ended. I'm not asking that others not celebrate — I simply want a basic acknowledgement of harsher realities like mine, to not have these painful words inflicted on me. Why is this part of being a church? Would Jesus have gone around wishing women 'Happy Mother's Day?' It seems absurd.

Happy Mother's Day.

No matter how satisfied I am with my own mothering ability, no matter how much my kids continue to affirm this, my reality will never fade away: the word 'mother' itself is increasingly a reminder of intense pain, and the very opposite of happiness. For everything my children have, I did not have. The joy I have in knowing I laid the foundation for their happiness does not cover over, or make up for, my own loss. It doesn't make it go away — it highlights it in still starker relief.

And if I, who had such a poor model for motherhood, and who had so few resources to call on for help, — if I managed so well, what excuse was there for my mother?

Mother's Day when I was growing up just meant our mother dropping loud hints that her favourite perfume was Ma Griffe. I assume Dad bought it for her. There was no-one saying, 'I love you, Mum', no conversation around the relationship the day is supposed to celebrate. Mother wanted perfume, and that's what she got.

I looked up the background of the perfume.

Ma Griffe not only means 'My Signature' but also 'My Claw', like an affirmation of strong personality and power but also a warning: 'don't mess with me!' The assertive character is expressed by both name and smell..[*]

I've never liked, and for decades now have never used, any perfume.

---

[*] https://www.fragrantica.com/news/The-Four-Lives-of-Ma-Griffe-A-Comparison-6401.html

TIME WARPS

'Trauma survivors live with a difficult phenomenon that is sometimes referred to as "trauma time." Trauma Time is a phenomenon that has grabbed and deceived almost every survivor of trauma at one point or another. Traumatic memories are stored differently than normal memories. They are encapsulated in unmetabolized form in the limbic, or emotional region of the brain — an area of the brain in which time has no meaning.'

— Debra Wesselmann: 'Trauma Time',
debrawesselmann.com

Time does strange things in therapy, my therapist says. One session, we agreed on an earlier time, as a one-off. I failed to make the change properly in my phone calendar. The therapist rings ten minutes after I'm supposed to be there. I rush, we have half a session, I feel awful and uncomprehending. I'm usually good at being on time and putting times in my calendar. On the way home I'm weepy. I remember my mother being angry at some misunderstanding over picking me up. She'd gone to get me, but I'd walked home. It happened again: I got home to find her gone. I burst into tears, telling my big sister I was worried our mother would be angry. But strangely, when she walked in the door, she was fine about it, smiling, okay.

The inconsistency was worse than consistent anger. It was the proverbial walking on eggshells, never sure what reaction your actions would get.

I begin to appreciate how important the seemingly little details are about psychotherapy. Always the same time, the same day. There's never any wait time. Your spot is held sacred. Always lots of notice for any change. It's a safe container, consistent, predictable; vital stuff for a traumatised body that didn't get this as a child.

We talk it over, my reaction. The therapist asks if I'd like a text on a day when the time has changed, or the day before, or an email. I ask for a text on the day. I put two extra reminder alerts on my phone for each session. I don't trust myself anymore.

One day, she shares some words of wisdom from her supervisor.

'Transitions are important. They are the therapy, really. How you come in, how you go out. I've noticed that you don't seem to welcome my warm small talk at the door when you come in and go out. Have a think about what you need in those spaces. There's no rush to tell me.'

At the door, on the way out, she says she feels like crying at the thought that the warm farewells she wishes to send me away with are landing wrong for me.

The next week, I ask for more space at the door, on coming in.

Week after week, for months, I'd felt uncomfortable, crammed into a small entryway with her holding on to the door. We try it. It feels much better, at first. I exclaim I can't understand why it took me so long to make such a simple request.

'You weren't asked about it,' she wryly comments.

But as the weeks go by, I notice, slowly, that the new arrangement is not right either. Now the door is opened, she says hello warmly, but quickly steps away, and moves to her seat, waiting for me. It feels too far away. I have to take off my shoes, and the eco-friendly sneakers I wear seem to take forever to remove. I feel lonely.

It takes me over three months to acknowledge this.

I come to her door once more, nervous. As I walk up to it, I've been saying over and over, like reassuring a small child: 'She's a nice person, she won't hurt you, you just have to ask....'

I knock, she opens, greets, and turns to go.

'I've been thinking,' I hurriedly ask, and she turns back, curious:

'I'd like you closer please, when you're so far away waiting for me to come over, I feel a bit sad.'

Her face lights up. 'Of course! Where — here — is this okay? And for going out — the same too?'

'Yes', I say, eyes focused firmly on taking off my shoes.

Movies lead us to believe that therapy is all about the big moments, the dramatic breakthroughs, the big memories, the big revelations, the sobbing and yelling. But the biggest deal can be in the smallest things, in my therapist simply noticing and saying aloud my barely recognised discomfort on coming and going. Her heartfelt, simple recognition that I cannot take in the good. Her readiness to change her normal practice, just for me, even when I am unable to ask. Her concern that I *feel* safe, knowing it's not enough just to say that I am.

In one session I confess I've been imagining the worst again, catastrophising that I'll end up in a psychiatric ward. My therapist sits a bit more upright, leans forward a little, looks me in the eye and says firmly: 'Robyn, you're not bad enough for a psych ward. And even if you were, because you have family support, there would be no place for you. They don't have the room. You won't go there.' That is the last day I remember having such fears. I needed to hear it out loud.

In another session, I talk about how hard it is to sit down at the start and look her in the eye.

'What would you like to see happen? What do you need?'

I'm flummoxed, again.

'It's okay not to have an answer,' she reassures. Which is good, because how do I know what I need, when all I knew in childhood was its absence? Whoever, aside from my husband at times, has asked me what I need like that? Or more crucially, is that not what good enough parenting looks like... to ask ourselves over and over, what does this child need of me, and how do I give it to them?

'Robyn, when the day comes that you breeze in here and start engaging at will, then that is the day our work in therapy is done.'

I must have looked slightly stunned.

'That doesn't have to be for a while yet,' she hastily adds.

I talk about an Instagram post I've seen, on shame. Shame as the root of all insecure attachment. Shame that tells us we must hide parts of ourselves, parts that aren't acceptable, our child emotions of pain and distress and inconvenient joy. Our work is to put words to it, bring it out in the open, because when shame no longer has to hide it can be worked through and begins to lose its power.

My shame is the shame of being seen as weak, for having emotions, for being incompetent, unable as a child to do the adult things that need doing when the adults don't do them. My shame is having adults who can't do their job.

Shame doesn't have to be about self-hatred, terrible self-esteem, and harsh self-criticism. It's as much about having to stay unseen to be safe, having to hide away the messiness and needs of my human nature to appease my parents, on whom my child-life totally depended.

I CAN FORGET

*'Give me a memory
I can forget...'*

— Tami Neilson song, 'I Can Forget'

In the ghostly battle of childhood trauma, sometimes things lurk at the edges of my brain, some things I shrug off, don't want as part of my identity. It's easy to keep it to the side; there's so much else to deal with in therapy already.

But something inside whispers, is there any *more* trauma?

Is there more sexual abuse?

Are there any more repressed memories?

Twenty months post-election loss, twenty-six sessions under my belt with my therapist, I'd felt like things were starting to shift. We'd discovered that I have a super low tolerance for emotional distress. Any trigger, any slight hint that I might be unseen, my inner reality not acknowledged — any of that sets me off. I become fuzzy headed with dissociation, stare into the distance or the floor; if it's severe, I shut down, barely able to communicate or move. I shared that one day I went to have a shower, only to feel in shock that my towel was already damp. I'd just had a shower. I couldn't remember it. Another day I sat and tried to do some Lego. I stopped, confused, as the two bricks in my hands wouldn't go together. I looked down and realised I was trying to put stud sides together, the wrong way round. I had gone AWOL, disconnected from my very body.

But with her encouragement, I'd brought in my writing, and we'd begun the long slow task of trying to connect my experience with my feelings. Things I'd easily type up at home on the laptop with no concern at all eerily turned into a portal to an unfamiliar experience of feeling emotions, the moment I looked down at the page in therapy. I'd print off a couple of pages, a section, a memory of childhood often intertwined with the here and now life.

I look down at my typed page, hear the gentle firm encouragement.

'Go slow, Robyn. Don't rush it. Aim for embodiment, not intellectualisation.'

I take a deep breath. After several such sessions, it still amazes and takes me by surprise. Today it's the section about Mother's Day.

There's a rush, a wave of energy from head to toe. I pause longer that day between paragraphs, between sentences, on the edge of being overwhelmed, coached by the warmth and concern of the therapist just a short distance away, whom I still struggle to look at when experiencing emotion. My breath deepens and the world fades around me. I reach out for Ajax, feel his soft, fake, but reassuring presence. By the time I finish that section and put the pages aside in relief, he's pulled on to my lap. There's a huge sense of achievement in getting through this section, but I'm aware of my fuzziness and spacing out soon after I stop reading.

'Wow. There's so much material there, probably five hours' worth that we could deal with. I don't think you could cope with that yet.'

Therapy is going to be a long haul.

Then two days later comes a phone call.

'Robyn, I talked to Liz today,' says Lorraine. This is Liz's friend, who has stood by her, supported, visited, hosted me on my visits, listened, advocated, cared, when there was no-one else in the family to do so. One of life's true angels. Liz by now has been in residential care for over fifteen years. It's been a seriously long haul.

Multiple sclerosis in even its early stages is debilitating. Liz first noticed double vision, a wobbliness in her legs, in the 90s. In advanced stages, MS removes every vestige of human ability and dignity. My sister has been in a wheelchair all these fifteen years. She lost the ability to shower, to dress and undress, to roll over in bed at night, to get in and out of bed herself. Over the last year or two, she's lost the ability to feed herself, to do a jigsaw, and now she's losing the ability to hold her head up. And, at times, her conversation now includes clearly delusional material.

'Most MS patients end up in a neck brace,' Lorraine explains. 'I encouraged her to try, just to try, a really soft one.'

Then comes a long pause.

'Robyn, I'm not sure I should be saying this. You've come so far; you're doing so well…'

'It's okay,' I say.

I think I'm calm, but more likely, I'm so disconnected over this conversation about my big sister already. There's no feeling, just rational thought. It's unspeakably awful, her current condition. What else could be more upsetting?

'I'll be okay, I've got a great therapist. Go ahead.'

'I was talking to Liz about you and the family, just giving general news,' Lorraine says.

'I mentioned things that hadn't been handled well in childhood, that there was an issue with your mother. And then she looked at me and said, "And Dad." I thought, oh shit. I asked what she meant: I listened. Liz sat more upright at this point, alert, clear-headed, much more like the Liz I remembered of old than of lately... and she said that your father "interfered" with her. With all of you. I said I hoped it ended with her entering teenage years, but she said no, it didn't.... I knew she didn't have a good relationship with your mother, from way back. But I thought it was okay with your father?'

A tinge more sadness for Liz creeps into my awareness.

'Liz also said you're all adopted! That seems odd. I'll go look up her full birth certificate... she could be delusional on all of this...'

We discuss the nature of trauma memories, of repressed memories, of not remembering, of siblings not always recalling what happened even if the traumatic experience did happen to all of them. I describe the one memory I do have of being sexually abused, but by a family friend: a memory repressed until I was nearly forty. I know all too well I may not remember, in the conventional sense, anything else.

What scares me the most, if I can even be that honest with myself, is the total blankness. There's no instant denial; there's no sense that this could never have happened. There's.... Nothing. Surely most people would feel *something*, when they've been told about potential sexual abuse by their father. No matter whether it's true or not, the most disturbing thing to me now is that I seem beyond being disturbed. Maybe because everyone seems to expect something like this. If I complain about my mother to friends or therapists, at some point, I'm asked, 'What about your father? How did he treat you?'

So, is it true? There are the hints from my mother's inappropriate disclosures at times about her sex life: there's the shadow of a memory that sometime, years ago, maybe another sister mentioned that Dad 'did something' to her ... I think? Or was that the elderly neighbour? I do remember Dad having to help Tina as a teenager with bathing, that time she was so zombie-like with sedative psychiatric drugs. As for anything Liz experienced, given the fifteen-year age gap between us, there's no hope of a clue to her experience of abuse in anything I can recall.

I search my mind for a while. I don't *think* there's anything — I don't have triggers around certain scents, or styles of pyjamas, no special inhibitions around being touched: my husband bears little to no resemblance to my father, except in his slightness of build and determined faithfulness to not leave his marriage.

What is reality, then? Given Liz's advanced stage of MS, she has made statements that are easily seen as deluded, this last year. But she also still possesses a keen mind, a sharp intellect. And I've heard stories like this before — shameful family secrets, kept for decades, until a family member nears death, until they desperately need someone else to know their truth, their story, their reality.

Maybe the adoption story is her brain's way of coping with the overwhelm of speaking the other things, the true things, out loud. Maybe it would be easier, less unspeakable, to be molested by an adoptive father than by your own flesh and blood, your own father who loved you, carried you when your little legs grew tired, was the one you run to when hurt because your own mother won't deal with your hurts and needs.

I start listing off in my head all the evidence that our parents were biologically ours — my DNA test, that of others in our family tree on both sides, my father's early letters to my mother, my mother's writing about her four birth experiences for a university assignment I did. And then I stop. Because what's important here is not to prove Liz wrong on one statement while telling her she's right in all or part of the other: I know that I at least, and almost certainly all my sisters, were not adopted. But I cannot have anything like that certainty over the statements of paternal sexual abuse. And certainty may never come.

I suggest to Lorraine that I come up to visit, sometime when it suits, if Liz would like: that I would like to come, to see Lorraine herself. I hug Ajax most of that evening, feeling a little dazed, unsure who I can share this with other than my therapist next week, and my husband.

A daughter gets in touch that night with great news, and we video call.

I mention how much I needed good news today. At the end she says, 'I need to know — not the details — but what is your bad news, Mum? Otherwise, I'll just be anxious that you and Dad are splitting up!'

I laugh, shake my head, apologise. Without going into detail, I reassure her it is something from the past, something to do with her aunty, nothing that will shake her parents' relationship. I smile that this is where her anxious thought has headed to. I'm relieved, because even as a full-grown, independently living adult, she still needs the security of knowing her parents love each other and will stay together, and that seems healthy and normal. It shows me yet again that we've done okay.

Had my parents broken up in my adult years, I'm sure my reaction would have been so very different. I never understood, even as a child, why my father stayed married to our mother. If I had been the adult then, I would have wanted to leave.

Chillingly, a few weeks later I am rereading van der Kolk. A passage I skipped over last time now reads like it is written in flashing neon lights: there are studies showing an association between incest and autoimmune diseases.*

This in no way proves my sister's statement to be true. Nothing now can prove or disprove that.

Life must be lived this way: often, there is no proof.

It could well be true; I will simply never know for sure.

---

* Dr Bessel van der Kolk, *The Body Keeps the Score*, pp. 150–151.

MORE TESTS

'I wouldn't even call it mental illness — the face of mental challenges is evolving incredibly rapidly, and we don't have the institutions or infrastructure in place to deal with this.'

— Dr Alok Kanojia ('Dr K' from HealthyGamer): YouTube, 31 December 2024, @Psychology in Seattle

Two years post-election, and I'm still more tired than feels right. Still overweight. Still not feeling healthy. I go to my GP to ask for blood tests.

I haven't been in a year. I book a double time-slot — indeed, one look at my details on screen means the on-to-it receptionist offered one without me even asking.

I start to bring the doctor up to date.

'This is Ajax, my support dog — I can't have a real one.'

Ajax, reliable as ever, elicits a wide smile from the GP.

'I've been with a good therapist now for the last year.'

'Oh, through the community team?'

I stare.

'Noooo… that experience was so bad, my husband insists we will never go near them again.'

'Yes, I've heard it can be bad.' The GP's face looks deadpan.

'Bad?' I think. Maybe more like 'life-threatening'. And it seems like you haven't heard that psychotherapy is not on offer through the public system? Maybe the GP is thinking the team referred me on to someone, I realise later. I could be misinterpreting again, but also, it's not reassuring. I've been receiving treatment for a year, and other parts of the health system know little to nothing about how any other part works.

We move on to the tiredness, the sensation of feeling my heart muscles be uncomfortable at times, not pain, just discomfort. I'm asked a series of questions off the computer screen about tiredness. Clearly my tiredness is nowhere near serious enough to be medically interesting.

We're at the halfway point when a loud noise distracts the GP. There's a pause.

'Sorry, I just need to see if that's outside or inside.' The GP hastily leaves the room.

I hear the very loud, very distressed voice, over and over. The other voice in the interchange is not audible. But some responses can be guessed. A distressed person is repeating over and over and over...

'No-one cares! I have no one! Most people have someone, I have no-one! No, you don't care about me! No-one cares!'

My GP pops back briefly to apologise, but they'll most likely need to call the police.

I sit alone in growing horror. There's no choice but to listen. The volume is incredible.

'I've got a proper fucking mental illness! No-one cares! I'm triggered!'

First principle of trauma treatment, I think. Validation. This woman is being disagreed with, being told most likely by her doctor — and mine — that they do care about her. What they do not seem to understand is that this is only making it worse.

Her actual experience, what she is feeling and telling the whole world loud and clear, is that no-one cares. Instead of acknowledging that feeling and how distressing that must be, they're adding fuel to the fire by trying to 'fix' the situation — by saying that they care. What they're not prepared to fully sit with, what their client just told them: she's not experiencing life that way. She's not feeling their concern. How could she, when they're not concerned enough to get training in basic psychological first aid?

I reach out for Ajax and pull him onto my lap.

My GP returns, pale, apologises briefly, stares at the screen. There's no comment on what just happened.

'Where were we...?'

'Tests,' I prompt.

'Ah yes. Let's do your blood pressure'.

Blood pressure? I think to myself. Are you kidding? Whose blood pressure would be normal after five minutes of hearing that level of distress in the building?

'My first reading is usually high,' I comment, trying to get verbal acknowledgement of the distress we both are feeling. It doesn't come. Just a glance my way, a quick smile.

'Yes, we often need to do a second reading.' Or a third or a fourth in my case, I think to myself. I don't see the results, but the second one must be satisfactory: no further comment is made.

Blood tests are ordered. I go to reception to pay, wishing them a more peaceful rest of their day, leave the building, and at once hear the same sound again. The noise level is only slightly reduced. The same words are still being said, over and over, from one of two open doors of a police car. I can see the officer's legs swung out onto the asphalt, but not her.

'No-one cares!'

Later, I order a water-testing kit. High copper levels can do bad stuff to the liver. Some of my liver results were 'slightly elevated', enough for a second blood test in a few weeks' time.

Everything about our tap water is just fine.

I ask my GP for my iron levels to also be retested. On a normal range of 10 to 30, mine sits at 10. One point lower and it too would be in the red, despite no menstruation for a year and an iron-rich diet. Yet it is apparently of no concern; there has been no comment on it at all.

I feel a bit let down once more by our medical system, but by now, really, I should know better than to have high expectations of a health and well-being focus. The tests and ranges and their interpretation all zero in on acute or dramatically wrong things. I'm told after the retest that the liver numbers are heading downwards (though still in the red) and that everything else is 'okay'. My iron levels have gone up to just 13, after a month of taking iron supplements I bought online. I'm still more easily tired than I would like. But there's no checkback as to whether my experience of my symptoms has changed: the numbers know best.

I have a six-monthly phone consultation with my hormone clinic. My hormone levels are stable. We spend twenty minutes discussing the iron levels and how best to raise them, in detail. The nurse agrees: we're not after the minimal end of normal range here, but 'optimal'. From her experience, she'd like to see my numbers in the top half of the range, not the bottom.

AWARENESS

'The client needs a new experience, not a new idea.'

— Dr Rick Hanson, citing Dr Friedman: 'Using Attachment Theory with MASTER Therapist Dr Sue Johnson', YouTube, 15 May 2023, @Forrest Hanson

We can learn all the psychology, all the terminology in the world, read all the books, watch all the podcasts. But more awareness is not enough, more intellectual understanding is not enough, to change my traumatised brain.

I learn so many new words.

Freeze and fawn, not just fight or flight.

Attachment wounds, attachment types, shadow-work, window of tolerance, hyper- and hypo-arousal.

Triggered, activated, dissociation.

Depersonalisation, derealisation, suicidal ideation.

Sit with your feelings, hold space, felt sense, embodiment.

Hypervigilance, rupture and repair, transference and countertransference, re-enactment, impingement.

Adjustment Disorder, Developmental Trauma.

Complex PTSD, Borderline Personality Disorder.

Functional Neurological Disorder.

Inner child work, limerence, mentalisation.

Adverse Childhood Events (ACEs), transitional object, amygdala, Poly-Vagal theory, somatically based therapy.

Cassandra syndrome.

Bilateral stimulation.

EMDR, CBT, DBT, IFS, SE, TA, CM, OI, an endless alphabet soup of therapy modes.

The difference between counsellor, nurse, social worker, psychotherapist, doctor, psychologist, psychiatrist.

My therapist compliments me on how aware I am.

'Doesn't seem to help much,' I grumble.

'Oh, it helps,' she says, gently smiling. 'It helps a lot.'

STARTING OVER

'How do you want to do this?'

— iconic Dungeons & Dragons battle-ending phrase popularised by Matthew Mercer, Dungeon Master of 'Critical Role'

A long, focused conversation with someone's work colleague elicits a strong suggestion.

'You should do a doctorate. People start to listen to you, once you're a doctoral student. You know your stuff.'

I know I don't want to be a therapist, a health clinician. But I do want to make a difference. I want to share this hard-won knowledge. I was, once upon a time, a good academic student. But now?

The path from strong suggestion to enrolment takes six months but feels like a lifetime.

Thirty years after my last academic study, I decide it is time to return to university.

Like reaching out for help, a return to study is not straightforward.

The email to the academic recommended to me goes unanswered for weeks. I finally leave a voicemail. The response is quick, an apology, somehow my email got marked as spam, he hadn't seen it. Here are my suggestions, can't help you further, sorry again.

In the meantime, I contact another university. This email gets a response. An academic gets in touch. I'm asked to send further information, then we'd make a time to talk. I send the information. And wait. For weeks.

I leave a voicemail with a sense of déjà vu, receive another apology, and a time is set for a phone call the next day. The time of the phone call comes and goes. No call. I text after fifteen minutes. Finally, a call, apologetic, harried, with background noise. More information is promised to me. When it comes by email, it seems obviously not applicable to me. I don't have any formal or work background in psychology, medicine, or any form of health. Many postgraduate courses simply aren't appropriate. This academic is struggling to see where I fit in, but they're also simply struggling to fit in my enquiry around their regular work, and they sound stressed. Maybe this isn't the right place for me.

Back on the laptop, I search again. My old university now has a campus here in Wellington, for medical science. There is a department for Public Health. The website emphasises that a graduate of any discipline is welcome. There are four potential intakes a year, not just one or two. There's careful structuring to suit either those who simply need some extra knowledge and skills for the workplace, or for those hoping to do research at master's level.

I take up courage, find a phone number, and ring: I've had enough of electronic messaging. There's a slight tone of surprise on the other end. We now live in a world of emails and messaging and texts, all of which usually come before actually talking to someone. But it's a great conversation, and I feel very welcomed and reassured. This sounds like a good fit.

That feeling goes away once I try to cope with the actual enrolment process. The accounts to set up for websites, the forms to fill in, the mass of directions, the way nothing seems to fit this very bespoke course I'm signing up for. It's a long way from my undergraduate years of queuing in person, being alongside others in the journey, feeling like you're on an adventure, talking to a real person. My sense of being unseen grows. I get triggered, and nearly give up. I stagger on, think I've finished the forms, only to be rung a few days later by tech support. They can see my enrolment is incomplete. I'm baffled. He's baffled. It takes over half an hour to work out what happened. There's one page where I needed to scroll further down, but it isn't at all obvious.

The welcoming email for the course lands in my new student inbox. I read a few lines, and halt.

Whaaaaaat? Oh no... The course is now being held on the other side of town. It's been in the central business district, an easy half-hour commute on the train from my northernmost Wellington suburb, for two years now. I hadn't realised this was only temporary. Earthquake-strengthening now complete, they're back to normal. The commute will be sixty to ninety minutes each way, changing from train to the unfamiliar bus system. I'm shaken. I could drive, possibly, if I have enough energy, but the carparks in that part of town are only free for two hours or else $18 for a day pass, and our lecture will be a three-hour session. It feels marginal enough, difficult enough, starting university again. This feels too tough. I'm triggered.

My husband is on holiday for the first two weeks of my seven-week paper. He drops me off, but I say I'll navigate my own way home by bus and train. The unfamiliar is overwhelming: I stand at the bus stop on the wrong side of the road for a few minutes, until I realise my mistake. I get the unfamiliar bus, I rush to the train, I get on the non-stop express service by mistake. This one goes two stops past mine. I ring Andrew to come rescue me. It's been a long day. Just attending one lecture feels like a huge achievement. I'm shattered.

It quickly becomes clear that I've been lucky. Instead of unfamiliar research methods papers or, even more terrifying, the statistics-laden subject of epidemiology, I've started with a paper on the nature of politics and policymaking. There are several others my age doing the course, but they like most others have had 'real' jobs in medicine or in the public service, jobs which relate directly to public health. Being older has more benefits than I expect, though. A lightning-fast tour of New Zealand's political history is easier when you've lived through more of it than most. There's a reference to Muldoon, a prime minister in the 1970s and 80s.

'He was a drunken bully,' I comment. The lecturer nods knowingly, a twinkle in his eye, and encourages the class to go look up videos of Muldoon calling an unexpected snap election, drunk, slurring his words.

One of the readings for the first lecture is so obtuse it rivals anything I recall from my philosophy major. Feeling incompetent, I try to reassure myself. If I with a background in law, philosophy, and some low-level political experience can't do the readings, who else will? I turn to another reading and with huge relief see that all the others are much easier.

We're primed beforehand that class interaction is expected, along with doing the prescribed readings. We're asked to introduce ourselves in the first session, including any way we may have engaged politically — signed a petition? Walked in a protest? As I expect, I'm the only one with experience of being elected. By far the majority have voting as their sole political experience.

There are two assessments per paper. The first is a massive struggle. My mind feels like it's trying to rewire itself on the fly. I'm still so tired, I can only manage an hour or two in the morning, at first. I'm so glad I started: I'm even more glad I can do the course part-time. I appreciate the luxury of not being here for a career, either academic or in the health or government sectors, especially not now, when all the 'back-room' jobs are under threat from public service cuts. I don't expect anything anymore: I'm just trying to corral my reactions, move through the triggered days, take one thing at a time.

For the first assignment I battle with unfamiliar uses of technology. Who knew that the web version of Word won't let you do a global change of footnotes to endnotes? Why did I persist with an online reference-creation tool which felt inaccurate? I checked one especially difficult reference, from the parliamentary debates available online, with a reference librarian. 'Oh, that's a tricky one!' The reply goes on to explain her answer, a very different-looking reference to the one the tool had produced. A bit panicky, I realise with only days to go that all my references need reformatting. I don't have time to find another tool. The very tedious manual process takes me five hours for under thirty references. I've done it by far the hardest way possible. Next time I won't make the same mistake.

Next time, that precious energy and time is put into editing, not reference formatting. My mark goes from an A- in the first assessment to an unexpected A+ in the second. This feels dazzling.

Or am I just escaping again, as in childhood? Is this just the same old route, trying to be 'seen'?

'No-one else but me will really appreciate what you've done in achieving this,' my delighted therapist says.

I certainly hope so. I certainly don't want my fellow students to know what it's like to be triggered, to leap to thoughts of hopelessness, helplessness, and death when things are overwhelming. I don't want anyone to feel like I do, battling these ghosts of trauma past.

There is a week break between papers. I need a break. It has taken everything I have, to do that first paper. It's only the last two lectures that I manage to do the commute both ways on public transport. Those days are exhausting.

But then comes another phone call from Lorraine.

Once again, my sister Liz may be dying. Once again, she must go into hospital, a hugely stressful time for Lorraine as the hospital staffing isn't up to the job and the rest home has no staff to spare. Hospital patients are expected to push their call button to ask for help. My sister can't push a button, her hands are too shaky, and she is too distressed. She can't hold a drink. Lorraine is spending hours a day by her side.

On discussion it's decided I won't fly up just yet. The week goes by, Liz goes back to the rest home, there are many calls to and fro, paperwork is finally set in motion as medical staff belatedly agree that it is time for her power of attorney to kick in. It's official. My sister is now formally deemed incapable of making or communicating decisions about her own health.

The distress of this, inevitably, is triggering. My second postgrad paper is about to start. I seriously contemplate not doing it, but that would drag out the end date for the diploma still more. At this point my goal is to see what level of functionality I can achieve, and to get my reflections and research into changing our woeful health system into print, or into whatever form will help spark awareness and change. I decide at worst I can start the paper and then pull out, if my sister dies, if I need to fly up to see her.

At our coffee break in this paper's first three-hour session, we're led down to the kitchen area, down a back route in the building which goes past a glass-walled office. Stretched on the floor an arm's length away from us, behind the glass, are two full-grown, gorgeous huskies, Alaskan Malamutes, just like Ajax. I feel like home.

At our forty-fourth therapy session, I feel relaxed and confident. A+ for the last assignment helps a lot.

My therapist stares at me in wonder.

'I feel like this is the first time I've got to meet you, the real authentic Robyn, not the distressed and suicidal you....'

I risk a look at her face, I feel happy, but shy. This is me? I've arrived? I feel vulnerable, unsure, concerned.

'Is it okay, though? I'm feeling so good right now basically because I'm doing so well at uni — isn't that too performance-based?'

'I go by, if it feels good, it probably is. Don't over-pathologise it. Enjoy it!'

We discuss the bits and pieces of academic life, the unexpected prospects. She repeats often and whole-heartedly, face alight, how excited she is for me.

'You wouldn't have thought a year ago you'd be doing this!' she exclaims.

'So, just checking, did you miss not having therapy last week?' I'd cancelled, in case of having to go up to Auckland.

'Yes,' I try not to mumble in unnecessary shame, trying to keep at least some eye contact.

'It was a hard week with the start of this assignment... I had a nightmare on Monday night about missing this session.'

She doesn't linger too long or delve too deep, just acknowledges. I've noticed her therapeutic touch is always lighter, less intense, after any break. But I'm always so struck by how emotionally tiring it is, to be seen.

The second assignment for my Health Promotion paper, is 3000 words, divided into multiple sections with specific requirements. I realise that the start of new things is stressful and overwhelming to me, and triggering. This assignment means I must 'start' several times over. I struggle. I get triggered. On the back of the distress over my sister and an elderly friend spending time in hospital after an injury, it's too much. One day, unexpectedly, calmly, I go looking for suicide means. I open the drawer in someone else's house I have access to, knowing there's medication there, not knowing what sort, hoping it's the kind in my plan.

It's not. It wouldn't achieve my purpose. Just give me a stomach-ache.

The discovery is a weird mix of relief and disappointment and shame, and now I must tell my therapist. Just for a day or two, I've gone back to being actively suicidal. After the triggered, suicidal episode subsides, it feels weird. I haven't been this 'bad' in over a year.

We talk it over at the next week's session.

'Robyn, some people with the kind of stress about your sister would deal with it by having a couple of wines and a pizza... your brain defaults to, "I want to die" as a coping mechanism.'

Wine and pizza? Hell, yes. Why didn't I get that kind of brain? I want that. It sounds so, so much simpler.

'Healing is not linear.' My therapist repeats this often. Even my grown offspring remind me of this one. I need reminding. Every dip downwards feels like a catastrophic, unsurvivable failure: and afterwards I feel weak, and shameful. But it is just a coping mechanism, one I hope to eventually unlearn.

. . .

One year with the same therapist. Forty-six sessions.

I feel like this needs celebrating, so I bake the moist chocolate cake recipe, the one I always used for the kids' birthdays. I used to write the number of their birthday on top with one colour of M&Ms. I put a '1' on this cake in yellow, slice off two pieces and box it up. I know my therapist likes this cake. I'd taken a piece a few months back, from a birthday celebration.

'Cake! How wonderful! Two pieces — do you want one now?'

I decline, and think no more of it, as we dive into the usual routine of a therapy session.

The next day, while doing some writing, a text comes unexpectedly from the therapist. She's thanking me for the delicious cake.

For some minutes I feel my inner world rocking again. While this therapist hasn't made her rules as explicit as others have, I know the boundaries of therapy. More than that, I know I *need* those boundaries. Most therapists don't reply or only reply briefly to any contact out of session, only get in touch in between if there's a need to change session times or dates, never cross the boundary into normal friendship. I can feel my alarm bells ringing.

I decide to wait a bit before replying, to see if I settle down emotionally.

Later in the day, I text back:

'Could you make a note to talk about this text next week please?'

'Of course,' she replies.

My reaction fades, but there's some ruminating thoughts. I know she's a warmer and more friendly kind of therapist than most, but what was she thinking, texting me like that? I'm angry, a bit, but this fades quickly as I name this as just a rupture, and know she'll be committed to repairing the problem. What would have seemed like a life-ending big deal emotionally a year ago is now just something inconvenient and awkward to work through. And then the rest of life kicks in, with someone we know being unwell, and the stress successfully diverts my thoughts until the next therapy session.

She remembers and brings up the text early in the session. I hesitate a little, but I know it's important to get it out. I explain how I felt, getting a text like that from her. I need to know that therapy stays in the room.

'If gifts are a problem, I can stop doing that,' I offer.

'Often other therapists wouldn't receive gifts,' she replies, 'but I see it as part of our culture — manaakitanga. I don't want to stop you from giving such gifts. Part of the problem is that my other clients don't usually do this. But the gift is not the problem, Robyn; the problem was me not stopping to think how contact outside the session would affect you. I'm sorry for the distress I caused you. I won't do it again.'

She pauses, reflective. I had already done a brief update on my week.

'You don't seem to have been affected all week by it. You were looking okay when you came to the door today? That hasn't been the case in the past when we've had a rupture.'

I agree. This is a huge milestone. My emotional response is way more appropriate — more regulated.

We restart on my reading aloud from my writing. I've chosen for this session the passage on my childhood piano lessons, on me not being able to cry, of the memory of doing EMDR with safe containers, of the measles episode.

Tears come to my eyes.

'Can you name this feeling you get around knowing you didn't get what your kids did? Anger? Gutted?'

'Gutted... because you can't replace that kind of relationship when you're an adult. It's irreplaceable, a mother's love, a parent's love, a parent-figure.'

Somehow, I can look her full in the eye while saying this and have tears in my eyes.

Another milestone.

'This may or may not ring true for you, but I'm feeling anger, a sense of not being able to breathe, like your mother took up all the air in the room?'

I don't disagree, but that isn't the picture I'm getting right now.

'The image that comes to my mind is that we — my sisters and I — were cardboard dolls to her. You know, the kind you cut out and use split pins to join the limbs to the body, make them move how you like, put paper clothes on them. We weren't real people to her.'

The therapist's face is a picture of anguish and horror. 'Cardboard dolls!' she repeats.

'We couldn't have done this three months ago; you couldn't have handled it. I don't think you dissociated — much? — today?'

'I'm a little fuzzy now, but I think it was much less than usual, yes,' I agree. I know I curled my feet up, as she'd sometimes suggested, just to keep present, just to remind myself I'm here and now, not back then. I can look her in the face much more. I can, almost, cry. There are one or two tears. It's taken all these sessions, all her skill and consistency, all my persistence: for so few tears.

I delve into my chosen topic for an assignment. I choose to look at the health outcomes for childhood emotional neglect (CEN). It is staggering. The very first research paper I pull up shows an association between moderate levels of CEN, according to the Childhood Trauma Questionnaire, and brain infarctions in older age. The researchers had done autopsies on a couple of hundred dead people who had previously filled out the questionnaire. The association with the brain infarctions wasn't with physical or sexual abuse in childhood, or physical neglect, or emotional abuse. It was just with emotional neglect. Moderate levels of neglect, not even severe, gave a nearly threefold increase in likelihood of the infarctions happening.*

In other words, I'm at least three times more likely than a lot of people to have bits of my brain die off in older age — which is pretty much, anytime from now on — than someone with 'low' levels of emotional neglect in childhood.

It's sobering stuff, but there's no time to be scared. There's another assignment to finish.

Despite the triggering, despite wanting and searching for means to die; despite getting angry at the assignment structure and angry at myself for the struggle, I finish the second assignment. The first one got an A. I'm happy with anything B or above, as a B average is needed if I want to do master's level.

But while finishing up this paper, a totally unexpected opportunity unfolds: possible publication in an academic journal.

'This class has done well,' the lecturer says after the first assessment is marked. 'Anyone with an A grade might want to consider approaching me: we could see about getting your work published. It seems a waste to have it just filed away. It's publication quality.'

I'm flabbergasted. In my head I had expected no chance of publication in the academic world until doctoral level at least, a very distant prospect that may never be reached. So now, along with trying to finish writing a first draft of my book, I have an article to prepare over the summer break.

The end of year approaches. My therapist flags weeks in advance when she will be away, invites exploration on how this break feels. We try some more reading out loud, but this time my wary self is sensing mixed messages. Correctly or not, I get it in my head that the therapist sees this tool as a prop, as inferior to an

---

* Robert S. Wilson et al., 'Emotional Neglect in Childhood and Cerebral Infarction in Older Age', *Neurology* 79, no. 15 (9 October 2012): 1534–39, https://doi.org/10.1212/WNL.0b013e31826e25bd.

unstructured, 'organic' session. In trying to talk this through I feel once more like I'm a five-year-old, hanging my head in shame, having made the other person feel bad: the therapist says she feels like my bringing up this kind of feedback feels like I'm telling her off for something she's done wrong. From my perspective I can't see it. I feel like I've given every indication I can how much I appreciate therapy, her consistency, her competency, yet here we are again — I've unwittingly made someone else feel incompetent, and naturally this gets a negative response. What I thought was good practice as a client giving feedback on how things feel for me has messed up the one source of professional help I've trusted.

After the second to last session for the year, I decide that the impending four-week holiday break needs extending to five. I don't want to go back next week. I'm tired of being triggered, I'm tired of being a trigger. It's time for the summer break, I tell Ajax, as I sit and type up the last tweaks, thinking of who might be up for reading it, who I can trust to give feedback without overloading them. A family member speaks with concern that the outside world, the publishing world, may not see the value that I do.

It's worth the risk. I think New Zealanders need to know just how dire the health system is, now more than ever with still further health sector cuts underway since I attempted to get help. And people need to know how complex the trauma from childhood can be. But also, I need my story out there, to feel like I exist: because if no-one is talking about trauma, then I am excluded, on the outer, shamed for good. It is, a New Zealand writer puts it, existential.[*]

---

[*] *The Mirror Book: A Memoir*, by Charlotte Grimshaw (Auckland: Random House New Zealand Vintage, 2021).

A WIRE MONKEY MOTHER

'Shame is a central experience of being a dissociative survivor of trauma...
We are ashamed to need the attuned human relationship that we know will cure it, because we fear that no-one will want to give it to us.'

— Carolyn Spring: Instagram, 27 October 2023, @carolynspringwriter

There are some deeply disturbing experiments in psychology and trauma-related fields that speak to me as if through a loud hailer.

There's the Still Face experiment. In the mid-1970s, Edward Tronick presented results of this iconic experiment to a meeting of the Society for Research in Child Development. In the experiment, an infant is exposed to three minutes of their mother being non-responsive and expressionless. The infant tries to gain her attention back in various ways, then quickly gives up and becomes wary, then withdraws: face and body turn away from their mother, and their face has a withdrawn and hopeless expression. This is still one of the most replicated findings in developmental psychology.*

Watching the video for the Still Face experiment is sobering. The infant is so clearly affected after just a few minutes of a non-responsive mother — from her emotional neglect. What happens when this, or something very like it, goes on for months…. For years? Did I get the still face response too often, did the baby me simply give up? Or get consistently inconsistent responses?

There's the Strange Situation experiment. Another from the 1970s, Dr Mary Ainsworth's experiments with a child playing, while mother and strangers come and go, were a big contribution to the development of attachment theory.† This is now understood as impacting us lifelong, not just as children: it's become a trend on social media, talking about your attachment style, your partner's attachment style, how to gain a secure attachment in adulthood if you got lumbered with the insecure form. Mine is avoidant, or maybe disorganised. More labels.

And the cherry blossom experiment: male rats were exposed to the smell of cherry blossom at the same time as getting an electric shock: their offspring and the offspring of those offspring, the

---

* https://www.gottman.com/blog/research-still-face-experiment/
See also https://youtu.be/vmE3NfB_HhE
† https://en.wikipedia.org/wiki/Attachment_theory

'grandchildren', were not given any shocks and yet were jumpy and nervous with exposure to cherry blossom. This and other studies around epigenetics are still being debated. Thankfully research has shown the reactivity to the scent can be turned around by desensitisation.* I feel that living with complex trauma is like going through life in deeply suppressed expectation of that same painful electric shock, random, uncontrollable, capricious, and relentless, not knowing its source or how to stop the pain, other than to avoid every hint of a trigger: and therapy is mostly about desensitisation, because the trigger is relationships, not a specific, highly seasonal, easy-to-avoid floral scent.

By far the most harrowing to me is the infamous cloth mother monkey experiment. Headed up by Harry Harlow in the 1950s, this chills me. Not just as a deeply unethical way to treat monkeys — though it's hard to argue otherwise. Harlow separated baby monkeys from their mothers soon after birth and put them in a cage with two substitute 'mothers' — a mother-shaped wire cage with a feeding bottle, and a furry-shaped monkey model with no food. Prior to this, Western science in its wisdom assumed that babies bonded with their mothers or caregivers just because that's who feeds them. But Harlow's monkeys clung tight to the cloth monkey, not the wire monkey with the food. They would reach out for food, detach long enough to get food: but they bonded with the cloth monkey.†

Harlow did a series of still more awful experiments. Once bonded with the cloth monkey, he introduced a scary, noisy mechanical object right next to the baby monkey's cage. The undoubtedly terrified monkey went running to the cloth monkey for reassurance, not the wire monkey. He also made the cloth monkey do terrifying things, but the baby monkey would not let go, once bonded.

---

* https://www.bbc.com/future/article/20190326-what-is-epigenetics
† https://en.wikipedia.org/wiki/Harry_Harlow

Pictures of the experiment are haunting. It's too simplistic, but at heart, I feel I was raised by a wire monkey and partly attached to a cloth monkey — maybe my sister, who remembers with delight the privilege of changing my nappies as a twelve-year-old, who is often pictured carrying me, who left home, when I was five, to live far away. Mother took many photos. It felt like she cared more about taking 'snaps' than about being with us. No wonder I expect relationships to end but yearn for consistency and permanence. No wonder I'm surprised when, year after year, our adult children joyfully come home to be with us and each other, when they seek out a hug from me, reach out if distressed. I guess that's normal, or at least, it's healthy. It's nothing like what I knew.

My mother was a wire mother, not a real mother: providing food, meeting no emotional attachment needs, providing no safe harbour when terrifying things happen. My mother was herself the source of terror. Physically, an infant, a young child cannot leave home. So emotionally, I disappeared — to survive. It was not until after my collapse that I understood this was called dissociation. And shame. Because if your own mother cannot create the basic sense of belonging you need to function as a human being, then who can?

A PRIVILEGED LIFE OF TRAUMA

*'There are some things that time cannot mend.
Some hurts that go too deep.'*

– J.R.R. Tolkien: 'The Return of the King'

There is ongoing debate in online support groups.

Survivors of complex trauma bluntly ask: is healing possible? Recovery? What does that look like?

Recovery is the wrong word, really. What is there to recover?

Some trauma experts cling to the notion that there is a pure self, something which survives no matter what, the real 'you', not your trauma-conditioned brain-body.

This is impossible for some to see, and that is understandable.

Where the origins of trauma lie in childhood, the framework of before and after trauma is lacking.

If you develop 'classic' PTSD from adult experiences such as wartime violence or a bad car crash, you have, somewhere deep inside, a memory of safety, a memory of feeling well, a memory of life 'before' the disastrous event. The memory of the event itself is trapped, unprocessed, and makes you relive the fear and helplessness over and over: but treatments such as EMDR may take only a handful of sessions to deal with the traumatic memory.

There is no such luxury for a child of trauma.

There is hope. There is the possibility of neurological change in our modern scientific understanding where once such change in adulthood was considered impossible. Neuroplasticity is the new buzzword. But this change is a fundamental reset of infant brain development, and it is an interpersonal neurobiological phenomenon: it requires a commitment by another human being to listen, be curious, love, and support you in a way well beyond anything normally asked of a friend or partner, and for a long, long period of time. This is financially, emotionally, and physically expensive.

The uniqueness of the parent–child bond makes it irreplaceable. You can learn to be that 'parent' to yourself, to make sure you give yourself the food and clothes and showers and compassion and opportunities for human connection that you need: you can accept parent-like attention with strict boundaries from a skilled therapist, you can accept, if you are incredibly lucky, the support of a healthy partner, family, or a friend that approaches the level of parental commitment to your well-being. But it will never completely fill the gap. The grief of neglect cannot be erased even by the best possible scenario in adulthood, by the best relationships. The trick is to learn to build a life and self around the void, without pretending it isn't there. You don't have anything as concrete as the proverbial elephant in the room, only a looming shadow of one. The work of healing is to draw a line around it, define and acknowledge it with someone else, and to try to build fresh ways of seeing the world. All while feeling terrified or numb.

On a global level, on a national level, the biggest problem is that most survivors have access to none of the best-case scenario resources.

It's not scientific, it's just a snapshot, my two years I've spent on Facebook groups and Reddit, YouTube and podcasts and blogs and survivors' published memoirs and listening to therapists with thirty, forty or fifty years' experience in trauma. But all this leads me to believe that childhood trauma wrecks most survivors' ability to have healthy relationships, leading to isolation or a series of abusive, toxic relationships. For most survivors, it ruins or seriously impedes their workplace opportunities, their ability to gain financial and housing security. Many survivors cannot escape the grip of a toxic family environment, through financial or other dependence: or if they do escape, they carry the grief of going low contact or no contact forever and then also experience the condemnation of their culture, their wider family, their friends. Often, they are not believed, even if they find the courage to tell their story. Often, they are retraumatised by health professionals, institutions, and systems that are in denial themselves.

Very few trauma survivors have my experience of being quizzed by therapists, puzzled, unfamiliar with a client who has a thirty-plus-year happy marriage. My guess is that the low self-esteem and negative self-talk that most survivors experience leads to super unhealthy relationship dynamics. I'm not saying I've had the perfect marriage or been the perfect partner or have a perfect partner: but what I do experience is commitment, compassion, communication, kindness, and respect, beyond the wildest dreams of many.

No-one wants to face the pain of trauma, but without the pain being fully seen and known, it cannot heal. 'Healing from trauma is more painful than the trauma itself,' says one psychologist/survivor.[*]

There are commonly used sayings in the trauma community of experts and survivors.

'Healing is not linear' (my therapist, among many in the field of trauma).

'This is an excruciatingly slow process' (my therapist).

'Emotional neglect *is* abuse' (Kati Morton[†]).

'Be curious, not judgemental' (Kati Morton again).

There's one that needs some nuanced understanding:

'There are no trauma Olympics.'

Comparing your own traumatic events to those of others will inevitably lead you to feel like a fraud, to think that others have it so much worse, to feel like others deserve help more. And yet, how else do we find out that our childhood was so dysfunctional, except by comparison with others? And how about a growing recognition of the especially insidious nature of a child traumatised by emotional neglect? That this kind of neglect is abuse, it is as bad as abuse, it is in some ways worse than abuse: harder to spot, easier to hide, easier to deny? It is inherently tough to understand neglect without comparison.

---

[*] Dr Ingrid Clayton: 'The Untouchable Mother - Believing Me, Healing From Narcissistic Abuse with @IngridClaytonPhD': YouTube, 23 February 2024, @Patrick Teahan

[†] Kati Morton: YouTube, Ask Kati Anything episode 192 at 21:34: https://youtu.be/TAjpwe6VeBw

One Instagram account describes the pain of a trauma survivor's grief as some of the most unbearable pain you might go through.*

Pete Walker describes complex trauma as 'more severe' than PTSD.† His later reflection on emotional neglect tells me just why books like his on complex trauma don't resonate enough with me. He writes of his repeated regret that he didn't know enough about the terrible consequences of emotional neglect, his resulting focus on other abuse in childhood trauma. Clients would come to him, minimising their childhood experience, just because they hadn't been physically hit like he had, when 'by far the worst thing that happened to me, by far, was growing up so emotionally abandoned': because recovery demands our facing the source of the pain, 'the great emptiness that springs from the dearth of parental loving interest and engagement, and around the harrowing experience of being small and powerless while growing up in a world where there is no-one who's got your back'.‡

So, where to from here?

I have learned I can trust and mistrust my memories, both at once. Some things I will never 'remember'.

I have learned how precious it is, how extraordinary it is, the remembrance of an ordinarily happy childhood, the memory imprinted deep into a child's very body, the love that discovers rather than creates a person, the vision that sees things no other will take the time to see, and yet still loves.

It is a memory I do not have and that no-one can give me, a pain that feels bearable only after it first is allowed to reveal itself and grow big, only when told to compassionate, ever-patient witnesses: it is a story that must be not only told but faced, layer by layer, not head on. It is a void that cannot be filled, only contained

---

* Instagram: @cptsdfoundation
† Pete Walker: 'Complex PTSD: from Surviving to Thriving'
‡ Pete Walker: 'Emotional Neglect and Complex PTSD':
https://pete-walker.com/pdf/emotionalNeglectComplexPTSD.pdf

and drawn into a fuzzy-outline silhouette in my being. It isn't all of me, but it is still a huge part.

I cannot remember something that didn't happen. I can take a clear look at my survival response, my denial. It took more than half a lifetime and a complete breakdown to bring myself to face how much I was impacted by the emotionally neglectful parenting of my childhood, the sexual abuse known and possibly unknown, and the lack of any other adult, protective, supporting relationships that every child so fundamentally needs.

The solidity of self still escapes me, and under pressure, the trauma responses of shut down, or of intrusive, catastrophic, and suicidal thoughts are still there. Their impact is lessening. There is no guarantee those responses will ever fully disappear, for me.

My therapist has other clients like this, clients she says have had suicidal thoughts all their lives. When I first heard that, I shied away from that reality.

I think my therapist hopes for more than that, for me. But, for now, the outcome is unknown.

And I'm okay with that. I know now. It's not about being fixed. It's about learning to be seen.

It's not an event to be reached, something to be achieved, finished, a box to be ticked off: it is a process that does not end.

It's about seeing and valuing all the trauma responses, the suicidality, the overexplaining, the overperforming, the putting others' needs first — all these responses, valued skills that helped protect me, helped me survive. They are not obstacles, a 'problem', or the enemy. This disconnect, this lack of feeling, must be itself felt and acknowledged: feeling what current reality is, not what I would wish it to be. A day-in, day-out practice of noticing the here and now, of asking what my body needs right now, to feel a little bit more secure, nothing too fast, just a little bit, always knowing the path doesn't head straight onwards or upwards at a constant rate.

Understanding and awareness aren't enough. I could — I hope to — write a master's thesis on trauma. That kind of awareness I hope will help others: awareness is a first step. But it will not heal me.

One day, perhaps, the tears will fully flow and not be checked or wiped away.

I do not want them wiped away, once they come. I don't want them fixed.

I prefer 'not all tears are an evil', to 'He will wipe every tear from their eyes.'*

---

* Gandalf's words, on the sorrowful parting with Frodo from his friends in Tolkien's *The Return of the King*: versus the oft-quoted words from the New Testament, Revelation 21:4.

POSTSCRIPT

I have recorded some things here that no-one outside the therapy room has yet heard. They are distressing, I think. But I am yet to be able to feel that.

Sitting in our seventy-first session together, my therapist looks at the mock book cover I've given her, with a photo of me as a child on the front. I found the class photo from the same year — it was Standard 4, so I would be nine at the start of that year. My therapist gasps in delight, commenting on how she's drawn to the child, how she wants to know her more, how common it is for a child to be smiling to the world but with turmoil going on within. She places her hand on her heart, clearly moved with emotion that I cannot feel. Yet.

I look back and wonder, did that really happen to me? Some days it seems like another person, another life. My therapist sees this as good and bad: good, because of the healing it shows. I'm no longer as distressed, no longer in the same kind of acute pain. But 'bad', or difficult, because I need to bring all this experience together. It is all me, it all needs to be integrated into the one life I live, the one narrative with so much that was unexpected. Knowing and telling and feeling your own story is not an optional extra.

Sitting with friends, so often today I hear them sadly describe conversations with their grown-up offspring, telling them of the hurtful things from childhood, the ways they failed their kids: often in ignorance of things such as how to deal with neurodiversity. I light up in reply. 'That's amazing — you've done such a good job! Your adult child actually wants to have a difficult conversation with you? They want a relationship with you. Do you see how precious that is — what if they never told you, never wanted that conversation, never thought it would be safe to approach you?' If I remember in time, I also acknowledge how hard it feels to hear that you've been a source of hurt for your child.

I could tell more. More memories: two occasions of child-on-child sexual abuse, the abysmally awful school ball episode, spiritual abuse by a pastor, leaving my first job in a fit of anger. More current challenges. Hearing about more abuse. Learning to talk with a delusional family member. Walking out of a therapy session in anger. Pulling out of a compulsory paper for my diploma, overwhelmed, triggered, but finally able to cry in sadness. Being unable to sit a test on the appointed day, spending the morning in exhausting shame, savouring the small victory of not being suicidal. The search for a psychologist who can diagnose levels of dissociation. Struggling to understand relationships. Struggling to get together a sustainable exercise programme, now that I'm at elevated risk of cardiovascular disease.

The story doesn't end with the close of this book.

This is my journey. It is not the story of other survivors of trauma, though there may be similarities.

May you be curious, may you have compassion not judgement, may you find peace.

ACKNOWLEDGMENTS

To those I have already thanked in person, I cannot name you here: you know all too well what you did to help bring this book into being.

I am grateful for the opportunity to learn so much and be comforted by the curiosity, compassion, and expertise of others, especially those who have shared online. To Kati Morton ('Ask Kati Anything'), Forrest Hanson, Rick Hanson (the 'Being Well' podcast), Dr Mike Lloyd of the CTAD (Complex Trauma and Dissociation) Clinic, Carolyn Spring, Nate Postlethwait, and others of this digital world, my deepest appreciation. To the experts and clinicians who have had their speeches and interviews recorded for years now, who have written books with the public in mind and learned from their decades of research and above all by listening to and believing their clients: to Dr Jacob Ham, Dr Bruce Perry, Dr Bessel van der Kolk, Dr Gabor Maté, Dr Diane Langberg, and others, thank you.

I thank the Public Health and support staff of Otago University, for their consistent encouragement and accommodation of this oft-triggered trauma survivor, and who do their work with such compassion and humility.

I am grateful to the online survivor communities I have been in, those who are traumatised and those who mourn a loss, and those who I am privileged to meet with in person or by video call. Redditors of the trauma groups, I acknowledge you. Again and again, we have told each other how terrible it is that you are here too, but how helpful, how much less lonely it feels, how much better it is to know that someone else understands. We all have different responses and yet so many are the same: the physical symptoms, the 'How are you?' greeting hatred, being light sleepers.

May we all sleep in peace, one day.

BIBLIOGRAPHY

Books by health professionals

Dr Sarah Woodhouse, *You're Not Broken: Break Free From Trauma and Reclaim Your Life* (Penguin Random House Australia, 2021).

Dr Bessel van der Kolk, *The Body Keeps the Score: Mind, Brain and Body in the Transformation of Trauma* (Penguin Random House UK, 2015).

Dr Gabor Maté and Daniel Maté, *The Myth of Normal: Trauma, Illness & Healing in a Toxic Culture* (Penguin Random House UK, 2022).

Dr Lindsay C. Gibson, *Adult Children of Emotionally Immature Parents: How to Heal from Distant, Rejecting, or Self-Involved Parents* (New Harbinger Publications, Oakland, California, 2015).

Dr Jonice Webb, *Running on Empty: Overcome Your Childhood Emotional Neglect* (Morgan James Publishing, New York, 2014).

Bruce D. Perry, Maia Szalavitz, *The Boy Who Was Raised as a Dog: And Other Stories from a Child Psychiatrist's Notebook — What Traumatized Children Can Teach Us About Loss, Love, and Healing* (3rd edition, Basic Books, 2017).

Kati Morton, *Traumatized: Identify, Understand, and Cope with PTSD and Emotional Stress* (Hachette Books, New York, 2021).

Elizabeth K. Hopper et al., *Treating Adult Survivors of Childhood Emotional Abuse and Neglect: Component-Based Psychotherapy* (The Guilford Press, New York, 2019).

Memoirs & others

Sheryl Sandberg and Adam Grant, *Option B: Facing Adversity, Building Resilience, and Finding Joy* (Penguin, 2019).

Bruce D. Perry and Oprah Winfrey, *What Happened to You? Conversations on Trauma, Resilience, and Healing* (Pan MacMillan UK, 2022).

Stephanie Foo, *What My Bones Know: A Memoir of Healing from Complex Trauma* (Allen & Unwin, 2022).

Tara Westover, *Educated* (Random House, 2018).

Jennette McCurdy, *I'm Glad My Mom Died* (Simon & Schuster, 2022).

Nellie Bly, *Ten Days in a Mad-House* (Dover Publications, 2019: originally published 1887).

Mark Wolynn, *It Didn't Start With You: How Inherited Family Trauma Shapes Who We Are and How to End the Cycle* (New York, Penguin Random House, 2017).

Gary Trosclair, *I'm Working on it in Therapy: How to Get the Most out of Psychotherapy* (Skyhorse Publishing, New York, 2015).

Megan Devine, *It's OK That You're Not OK: Meeting Grief and Loss in a Culture That Doesn't Understand* (Sounds True, Boulder, Colorado, 2017).

Charlotte Grimshaw, *The Mirror Book: a Memoir* (Random House New Zealand Vintage, Auckland, New Zealand, 2021).

Podcasts and other online resources

Kati Morton: *Ask Kati Anything*

Episodes 1–179 were originally posted on a different channel; visit https://www.youtube.com/@OTDM/podcasts

or the playlist on the @Kati Morton channel: https://www.youtube.com/playlist?list=PLMSjrqhPvOoZrz95tshKA9tIymbqxNxKn

Forrest Hanson: *Being Well*, YouTube: especially —
Complex PTSD in 5 Minutes (26 November 2022)
https://youtu.be/MhAx-4ncSik
Recovering from Complex PTSD with Elizabeth Ferreira (20 June 2022)
https://youtu.be/FHRgPA_jagE
What Really Helps Trauma? | Dr Jacob Ham (21 November 2023)
https://youtu.be/uqcNYfQtbFw

Dr Mike Lloyd: *The CTAD Clinic*, YouTube: especially —
10 Things That Make Getting Through a Dissociative Day Harder (19 February 2024)
https://youtu.be/NSB_KVZR1ws
Dissociation and Timing (3 March 2024)
https://youtu.be/EG1eqNH3fzc
The 'Therapy Trap'...and how to get out of it (6 May 2024)
https://youtu.be/jgjEx6FuWJw

Carolyn Spring, www.carolynspring.com: especially —
https://www.carolynspring.com/blog/why-the-symptoms-of-trauma-make-sense/

Nora McInerny: *Terrible, Thanks for Asking*: especially —
The Resilience Myth with Soraya Chemaly (18 June 2024)
https://open.spotify.com/episode/66bPTcLBnj7OcqlGcZIouP

ABOUT THE AUTHOR

Robyn has degrees from a long, long time ago in law and philosophy, in the days when essays were handwritten and posted in person into the lecturer's wooden mailbox. She's done all the jobs in life she never expected and none of the mystical 'career' she always wanted: librarian, full-  time child-rearing, used car sales (electric only!), and local body politician. Married for thirty-five years with four grown offspring, she still lives in their first house with her first husband, their fifth cat James, faithful Ajax, and their first offspring. She's been instrumental in her suburb's first community garden, spoken numerous times to community groups, and been part of her city's first ever adult group for Lego enthusiasts. One of her happiest moments was carrying her first MOC (My Own Creation – not an official set – the gold standard of plastic creativity) into our national museum, Te Papa, for display in support of the professional 'Brickman: Wonders of the World' event.

Currently Robyn is studying at a snail's pace for a postgraduate diploma in Public Health, focussing on the lifelong impact of childhood trauma. Weekly psychotherapy continues.

Contact Robyn: robynparkinsonauthor@gmail.com

www.ingramcontent.com/pod-product-compliance
Lightning Source LLC
Chambersburg PA
CBHW031235290426
44109CB00012B/309